50 things heating professionals need to know about Heatpumps

Another simple guide to renewable heating.

Graham Hendra

Version 1 July 2022

David I hope
you enjoy this

Dedication

To everyone who bought book 1 thankyou, this is a continuation of the same subject.

To everyone who has ever thought they were asking me a "stupid question".

There are no stupid questions, it's stupid not to ask.

Preface:

I have worked as a technical support engineer in renewable heating for a decade and a half. I specialised in Air source heat pumps in the domestic sector. I joined this industry before it was cool to be in renewable heating and before the government here in the UK jumped on the bandwagon. I have experimented with this technology in my own house, and I am ashamed to say in the early days in our customers houses too. My team and I learnt a lot on the way, we have been cold and wet, we have been shouted at and held high on the shoulders of our peers at times. It's been a real roller coaster.

Over that time, I have been asked literally thousands of questions. I'm inherently lazy so to save me answering them again I chose the most popular questions and tried my best to answer them here. This book is designed to help with the most common questions asked by heating engineers

Heat pumps are not really very complicated once you strip away the jargon, so in this book I'm going to try to make the subjects easy to understand using analogies and stories which are easier to relate to. I've tried to keep the answers as simple as I can without wading into thermodynamics and mindless maths.

Hopefully this will be useful to installers, energy surveyors and heat pump deniers alike.

I hope you enjoy the results.

Contents:

51 What is a heat loss calculation?

51 How do I do a heat loss calculation?

52 Full explanation and example of a heat loss for a single room. Ventilation loss

53 Why do you need to know exactly how much heat I need; the boiler man can do this in a few minutes?

54 What do I need to know about a building to do a heat loss calculation?

55 Why do I need a heat load and an EPC?

56 What is MCS / How do I become MCS?

57 What is a performance estimate?

58 What is an MCS Compliance certificate?

59 What is MIS020, tell me more about noise? And Do I need planning permission?

60 Should the conservatory or garage be included in the heat loss?

61 If I have a separate annex can I claim the BUS twice?

62 What are all the accessories that come with my heat pump

63 Under floor heating how it works

64 Show all types of standard installations and what goes into them

65 What's a pre plumbed cylinder

66 Minimum system volume

67 Why is flow so important?

68 Why do we use a header, a plate heat exchangers or buffer? what is hydraulic separation.

69 What's the difference between primary and secondary flow

70 What happens if the flow is too slow or too fast?

71 What's a PWM pump

72 Thermal stores and heat pumps

73 What is a monobloc? The boiler in the Garden.

74 What is a split? - the unit comes in 2 pieces with the boiler indoors.

75 What's FGAS?

76 Can I heat the water to 50C with a heat pump and boost it to 70C with a boiler

77 do I need a plant room?

78 Can a heat pump go on the wall or roof?

79 If I live by the sea will my unit rust?

80 If I mount the heat pump on a South facing wall, does it work better?

81 Can I have more than one cylinder with a heat pump?

82 An alternative, Using 2 Cylinders in Series

83 Can the cylinder go in the loft? Can it be horizontal? And can it go outside?

84 If I have 3 flats, can I serve them with one heat pump and a single cylinder?

85 Do I need a backup heater or immersion heater?

86 How hot is the hot water? will I need to boost it with a heater? what are you doing about legionella?

87 What's a secondary return pump / Hot water re-circulation pump?

88 Do I have to change every radiator? can I move some radiators around? can I keep my rads and suck it and see?

89 Can a heat pump re-use the pipework in my house, or will I have to have all of it changed?

90 Does microbore work on heat pumps?

91 What's DNO and have I got enough power in my house?

92 Who is my dno?

93 Types of Supply

94 Load shedders and power limiters

95 Identifying my heating system.

96 What servicing will my heat pump need?

97 What is going to go wrong with my heat pump and who can fix it?

98 My heat pump has frozen up, who defrosts it?

99 What refrigerant is in my heat pump are some better than others?

100 If the refrigerant is flammable, will it be dangerous?

101 Why is my run cost higher in Winter than Summer?

51 What is a heat loss calculation?

Most of us want to live in houses which are nice and warm, something like 21 degrees C inside. The problem is heat likes to escape form the house, especially in cold weather, the heat slowly leaks through the walls, windows, floors, and ceilings.

To maintain the house at 21 degrees C we must replace the heat at the same speed its escaping. If we replace the heat too slowly the house cools, if we replace it quickly the house warms up.

Of course, we have all experienced this ourselves, if we turn off the heating on a cold day the house gets colder.

The rate at which the house loses heat is determined by a few factors, the first is, the bigger the difference between the temperature inside and outside the quicker the heat escapes. You experience this yourself, If you stand outside as it gets colder you get colder quicker.

The next factor is the insulation of the house, again you can experience this yourself, if you wear layers or a big coat you stay warmer longer. Your clothes are acting as insulation. We need to work out how much heat leaks out of your house so we can replace it at the same speed as it leaks out. This is a heat loss calculation.

If you take a thermal image of your house with a thermal camera you can see where the heat is leaking. Red is bad, blue good. Note how this house has very leaky windows and roof.

51 How do I do a heat loss calculation?

To do a heat loss calculation we have to measure every wall, window, door, floor and ceiling in the house, work out what the area of each one is and then calculate the heat loss through each one taking into account the insulation and the temperature inside and outside. Once we have done this, we add them all together to get a total heat loss. It could be very slow and tedious if we did this by hand, so we use tools to help us.

Here is an example of a heat loss doing it long hand:

We will do a heat loss on this box. Its 1m wide, 1m deep and 1 m high.

Inside the box its 20 degrees C, outside its 0 degrees C.

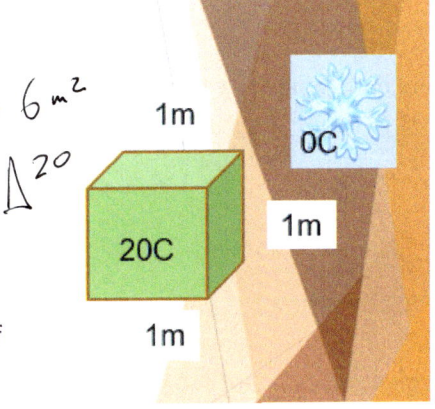

If the box is made out of good insulation not much heat would get through it, If it's made out of bad insulation lots of heat will leak through. Its leakiness is called the **U value.** U values are measured in Watts per metre squared per degree difference.

There is a formula

Q = u x A x ΔT

Q is the speed or rate of heat loss

U is the U value or insulation value; we look this up in tables or on google. If this box was made of double-glazed windows 2.8 Watts of heat would leak out of it if it was 1 metre square and the temperature difference across it was 1 degree C. If it was made of 100mm thick foam insulation only 0.22 Watts of heat would leak through 1 metre squared if there was a one-degree difference across it.

A is for the Area in metres Square, our box is 1x1 metres for each side, there are 6 sides so its 6m^2

The difference in temperature between inside and outside is 20C (we call this delta T) or ΔT

So, Q = 2.8 x 6 x 20 = 336 Watts. That's the heat loss.

The box is simple to do as its all made of the same stuff, but this isn't the case in a house. So, to get the total heat loss we look at one surface at a time. We literally work out the areas of all the walls, all the windows, the roof, and the floor separately. We calculate Q = u x A x ΔT for each one at a time and add them all together to get the total.

Now you can see why it takes so long, even with heat load calculation tools.

52 Full explanation and example of a heat loss for a single room.

Based on what we learnt in q51 we are now going to do a full heat loss for just one room of this house.

We will do this for the red room.

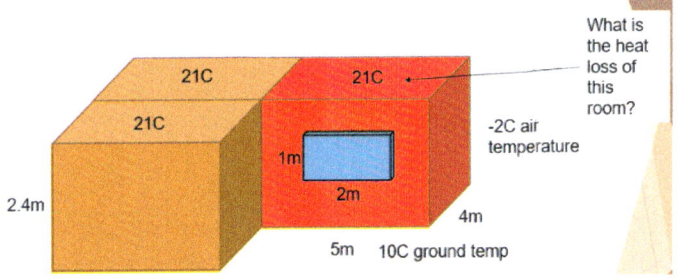

Firstly, we need to survey the room and list what we have got?

How many walls are external?

What is the area of the external walls?

What is the window area?

What is the roof area?

What is the floor area?

The walls, the wall on the left has no heat loss it's because the room next to it is the same temperature, if there is no temperature difference there is no heat loss, the delta T is 0.

All the other 3 walls do have a heat loss, its cold one side and warm the other.

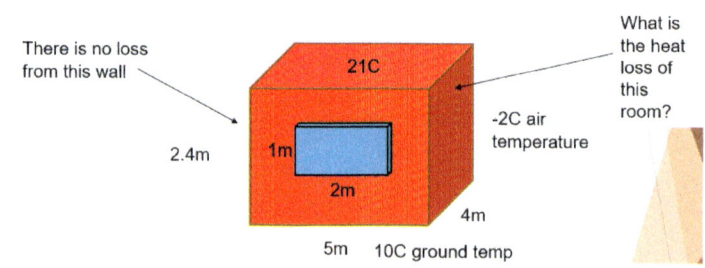

Next think about the window in blue on the front wall.

When we work out the size of this wall, we must subtract the area taken up by the window, it's unlikely that the wall and window have the same insulation properties.

Here are the U (or insulation) values for our house, we will use these for our calculation.

Wall u value=   1W/m^2K

Floor u value =   2W/m^2K

Ceiling u value =   3W/m^2K

Window u value =   2W/m^2K

To make the calculation easy to follow I have drawn a simple table up.

We are going to fill in each wall, floor etc one at a time. Give it a go.

Reference table

	length	width	area	U value	Inside temp	Outside temp	Delta t	Total Q
Floor								
Ceiling								
Wall								
Window								

We add up the total Q to get the heat loss.

Once we have worked out the Q or heat loss for each wall etc we add it together to get a final heat loss.

Answers:

	length	Width / height	area	U value	Inside temp	Outside temp	Delta t	Total Q
Floor	5	4	20	2	21	10	11	440
Ceiling	5	4	20	3	21	-2	23	1380
Wall	4 5 5 -2	2.4 2.4 2.4 1 total	9.6 12 12 -2 31.6	1	21	-2	23	726
Window	2	1	2	2	21	-2	23	92

2638

Here are the answers.

Note 2 points, the ground is not -2 degrees C, its warmer, so the delta t is less for the floor.

I've subtracted the window area of 2 metres square from the front wall.

It's interesting to see that in this house if you lay the information out in a table it's easy to see where most of the heat is leaking out. If I lived here, I would be putting some insulation in the ceiling.

Ventilation loss

In Q 52 we did a heat loss calculation on this room

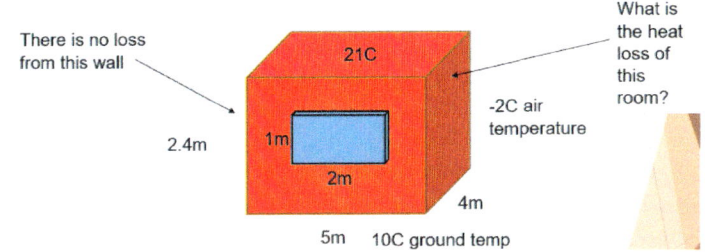

But this calculation only worked out the losses through the surfaces of the room. It didn't look at drafts or ventilation losses.

In all houses you get drafts, if you think about drafts from a heat loss point of view cold air leaks into the house and pushes lovely warm air out taking its heat with it. We must heat this freezing cold air up to make it comfortable, this heat is on top of the heat lost through the wall's windows etc. Therefore, drafty houses need lots of heat.

To work out the ventilation load we need to work out the volume of cold air that enters the room and needs heating up in one hour.

In new houses this is easy, an air tightness test is done on the house they put a fan in the front door, close all the windows and pump the house up, they can then measure how quickly the house leaks air. In old house we don't do this, we literally guess how much it leaks. **Here is the formula:**

First work out the volume of the room in m^2 (length x width x height)

We assume the air changes 2 x an hour in bathroom and 1 time per hour in bedrooms

Vent load Qv = Volume of room x number of air changes per hour x 0.34 x Delta T (inside temp – outside temp).

The 0.34 is just a factor we have to use. I will cover the psychometrics of air in a later book.

So Qv = 4*5*2.4*0.34*(21- - 2) = 375.4 Watts

We add this to the heat loss through the walls etc to get the total.

Air Changes ↓   *Fabric Heat Loss* ↓
Total heat loss is 375.6 + 2638 = 3013.6 Watts

In conclusion: our house leaks at a rate of 3014 Watts when it's very cold outside. We need to put a heating system in that can replace that heat at the same rate. If we buy a 3kW heater it will be able to heat the room even on a cold day.

You could do a further calculation; in this room it needs 3014 Watts to hold it 23 degrees above the air temperature outside. That means it takes 131 Watts (3014/23) to hold this room 1 degree warmer than the outside air.

If we buy a 2kW heater it will hold this room 2000 / 131 = 15 degrees above the air temperature outside.

When we are investigating problem sites where the heat pump is potentially too small this is the calculation we use.

53 Why do you need to know exactly how much heat I need; the boiler man can do this in a few minutes?

We calculate the heat loss as accurately because we can and try to size the heat pump as closely as we can to meet this load. If the heat pump is too small, we won't be able to get the house up to temperature on the coldest days see Q53. If the heat pumps are too big it's expensive to install and buy.

Boilers tend to be hugely oversized; most are 24 or 30kWs. You can't buy small boilers of 10kW, I assume it's because a 10kW boiler wouldn't necessarily make it much cheaper to buy than a 24kW boiler, so they are usually much too big for the job.

If the boiler is going to be massively oversized there is no need to do an accurate heat loss, so this is much less

heat load calcuator Grid
kWs

year / floor area	100m^2	150m^2	200m^2	250m^2	300m^2	400m^2	500m^2
pre 1918	12000	16500	20000	25000	30000	40000	50000
1918-1970	10000	13500	16000	20000	24000	32000	40000
1970-1990	9300	12000	14200	17750	21300	28400	35500
1990-2000	8400	11250	13000	16250	19500	26000	32500
2000-2010	6000	7500	8800	11000	13200	17600	22000
2010-2016	4600	6000	7200	9000	10800	14400	18000
2016-2020	3600	5250	6600	8250	9900	13200	16500
2016-2020 with HRV	2900	4200	5400	6750	8100	10800	13500

important.

As we can see from this table of approximate heat losses a 24kW boiler would be big enough for a Victorian house of up to 200m^2, a 30kW would do a 300m^2 house. In a new house a 24kW boiler will cover pretty much any size house.

Boiler engineers can size the boiler quickly.

54 What do I need to know about a building to do a heat loss calculation?

To do a full room by room heat loss on a house we need:

A rough idea **when the house was built**, this will tell us roughly what the house is built of.

A **floor plan** so we know where each room is, we need to be able to tell if there are heated rooms next to above or below the room we are working on. This is a floor plan; this sort of

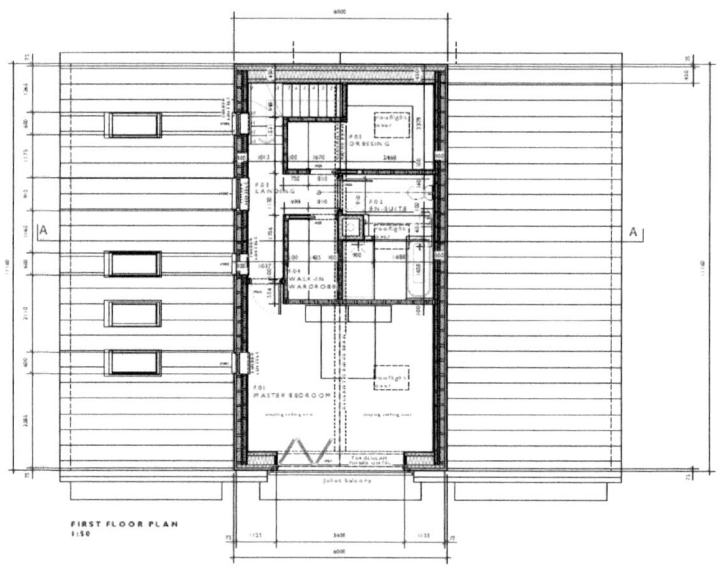

thing makes our life simpler.

A **description of the wall construction and thickness**, telling me it's made of bricks doesn't help, we need to know its bricks with a cavity block, plaster etc. If you don't know this is why we want to know how old, it is so we can estimate the construction.

Details of **the window sizes and construction** we need to know if they are single or double glazed, if they are plastic or wood etc.

Details of the **floor construction**, is it concrete? Is there any insulation under neath or is it wooden with air bricks?

Details of the **roof construction** and insulation. We don't really care about the roof itself, it's the ceiling of the rooms and if there is any loft insulation above it and how thick.

If there is any **mechanical ventilation**, in modern houses they are so well sealed up they literally have to bring fresh air into the house with a fan, if this is what you have in your house, we need to know the details so we can work out how much air it brings in.

And finally we need to know if you want to heat all the rooms, (garages etc).

55 Why do I need a heat load and an EPC?

We covered EPC in Q37 in the first book.

The EPC energy performance certificate works out the average heat lost through the year and makes recommendations how to save energy.

The heat load calculation works out the peak heat loss on the coldest day of the year.

The process of doing the calculation is very similar but they are looking at different things.

You cannot choose a heating system based on the EPC it doesn't have enough information. So, an assessor does all the measurements for your EPC and then another assessor comes to do a heat load calculation.

Its been suggested that both calculations could be done at the same time to save money and time but that's not normally the case.

56 What is MCS / How do I become MCS?

MCS is a quality control system designed to make sure the consumers have a positive heat pump (and other renewable technologies) experience. It protects the homeowner from the installer and vice-versa. It is designed to give consumers confidence that the job has been done properly and no short cuts have been made. It's now thought of as a badge of honour by installers, if you are MCS accredited you are a good installer.

MCS are the gatekeepers to the government grants like the Boiler upgrade scheme. Without MCS accreditation there are no grants.

MCS does not ensure a perfect installation, it makes sure the process is carried out to a standard procedure and correctly so it could be tracked in case of any problems.

MCS themselves say

"With energy costs constantly rising and climate change affecting us all – low-carbon technology has a bigger and bigger role to play in the future of UK energy.

We're here to ensure it's a positive one. Working with industry we define, maintain and improve quality – certifying products and installers so people can have confidence in the low-carbon technology they invest in. From solar and wind, to heat pumps, biomass and battery storage, we want to inspire a new generation of home-grown energy, fit for the needs of every UK home and community."

To become MCS accredited you must implement the MCS standard procedures into your business. There are companies that are set up to help you with this process. Easy MCS is the most used, they will help you get through the process and to become accredited. It costs a fair bit to do and takes a few weeks, its not a simple fill out a form and you are accredited.

You will be audited annually to make sure you are working the correct way.

57 What is a performance estimate?

One of the many forms in an MCS pack is a performance estimate.

The performance estimate is a form which the installer fills in to show the customer how much energy they are using now and how much they will use when there new heating system is installed.

It's supposed to give the homeowner an un-biased overview of their new heating system before they buy.

The format of this form is non-negotiable. MCS give you a template to use like this.

Heat Pump System Performance Estimate

Installer Project Reference	1234
Client Name	John Doe
Installation Address Line 1	123 High Street
Installation Address Line 2	Old Town
Installation Address Line 3	Home counties
Installation Postcode	AB1 2CD

Energy Performance Certificate (EPC) Information

Does this estimate relate to a new build or proposal for extension or reduction in size of an existing building?	No
EPC No. for building	
Energy required to heat property	25,000 kWh
Energy required for hot water	3,000 kWh

58 What is an MCS Compliance certificate?

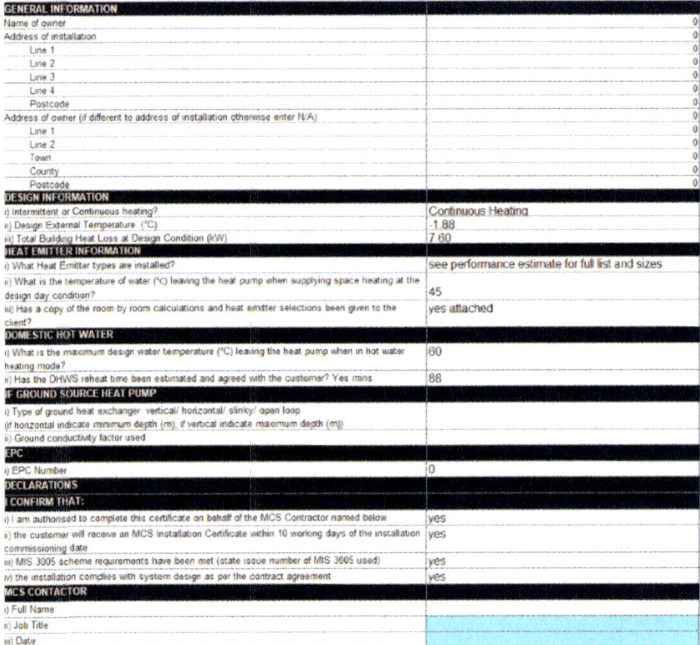

The MCS compliance certificate shows the customer what the heat pump has been designed to do, what temperatures it was designed to provide and how quickly it will heat the hot water. Its part of the MCS paperwork. It is another form which has a set layout, you have to submit it to MCS to tell them the system is installed.

59 What is MIS020, tell me more about noise? And Do I need planning permission?

One of the processes in MCS is to do a sound / noise test on the heat pump before it is installed.

You don't have to install the unit then see how noisy it is, that would be crazy, but what you must do is a calculation based on the unit installed and the distance it is from the neighbor's house.

If you can meet the criteria laid out in MIS020 you can install the unit without planning permission, if you fail you must rethink the installation and re do the calculations till you pass or need to go for planning permission.

- Here are the rules:
- You can only install one heat pump, if you install more than one you need planning
- The unit must be smaller than 0.6m^3 in size or it will fail, and you need planning.
- When measured from the nearest openable window of a habitable room (lounge bedroom etc.) of the neighbor's house the unit must be quieter than a calculated 45dBA.
- The unit and the installer must be MCS accredited.

This form has more influence on the system you are having installed than anything else. No one wants to go for planning permission as it slows the process so we all work inside these regulations.

The formula for working out the noise is quite complex, so everyone uses tools to do this.

All you need to know is the Sound power and the sound pressure of your unit and the distance from the neighbour's window to work out the noise level.

There are allowances if there are walls or fences between the heat pump and the neighbour.

As a rough guide most modern heat pumps can be installed 5-6m from the neighbour's house if there is a fence between them. Some super quiet modern units can be even closer than that.

60 Should the conservatory or garage be included in the heat loss?

You do not have to include unheated areas or rooms in the heat loss, we covered this in Q 42. If the area is unheated and has no heating system (radiators or underfloor heating) in it, you can exclude it from the heat loss.

Typically, garages are excluded.

If the conservatory is unheated and can be closed off from the rest of the house, it can be excluded. If it's open to the house, you need to allow to heat it.

I often add the unheated rooms to the calculation but note that I'm not heating them, it shows they have not been forgotten.

On estate agents' drawings they show the total floor area of the house, including garages etc so if they are in the heat load calculation but noted as unheated the total house area matches the estate agents floor area.

61 If I have a separate annex can I claim the BUS twice?

The BUS scheme which starts in May 2022 can only be claimed once for your house. If you have 2 boilers and replace them with 2 heat pumps you cannot claim twice. But under very specific conditions you can claim twice:

If you have a house with a separate house on the land its feasible that you could claim once for each house.

If the house is a maisonette, you could claim once for upstairs and once for downstairs. Likewise in a separate annexe you could also claim twice. It's because they have the following:

A separate postal address

A separate EPC for each building

A separate heating system in each building

A separate power supply to each building

2 separate energy bills.

If any of the above is missing, you can only claim once.

62 What are all the accessories that come with my heat pump

Feet, Flexi hoses/ Filter ball/ Flow meter/Robo-kit/ Low loss header/ Plate/ Fused spur/ Isolator/ Glycol.

Feet:

The outdoor units need to be mounted 100mm above the ground, we recommend using rubber feet with Unistrut channel. These come with mounting bolts included. They are 450mm long, 200 wide, 100 high and weigh about 10kgs each

Flexi hoses:

The water connections to the back of the unit are 1-inch BSP male. We recommend connecting the water pipework with flexible hoses for ease of maintenance and to avoid any vibration from the unit going into the house.

All external pipework must be insulated to meet MCS standards. The flexi hoses allow connection onto the back of the unit and then into standard 28mm copper pipe. They also allow the unit to be moved around a little for maintenance.

2 port valves

If you require domestic hot water and heating, we use electrically driven valves to direct the water to the correct place. Here you can see a two-port valve cut in half, the motor moves the little ball inside to stop the water or to let it go through. In our systems we use 2 x 2 port diverter valves one for heating one for hot water. They are always 28mm diameter.

A 3-port valve is similar but has 3 connections in a Tee shape, the middle of the T is open to either the left- or right-hand pipe all the time. The ball diverts the water one way or the other.

In our systems we use a 3 port diverter valves for heating and

hot water. They are always 28mm diameter.

Filter ball

In all cases a strainer needs to be installed in the return to the heat pump. The filter / strainer ensure that debris/foreign materials do not cause damage to the heat exchanger in the unit, voiding warranties. If dirt gets in the heat exchanger you get low flow and high-pressure faults. Traditionally we used Y strainers like this, they are brilliant, but you have to drain the system to get the filter out to clean it.

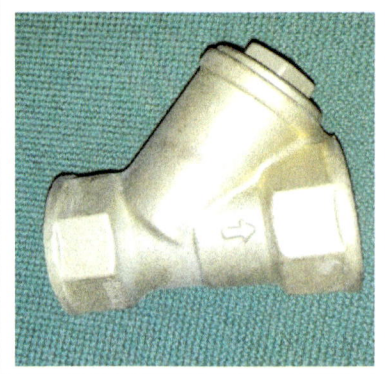

Nowadays everyone uses filter balls, it's a ball valve with a filter inside, to clean it you shut the valve, pull out the filter and you only loose spoonful of water.

Flow meter

Heat pumps have to have continuous uninterrupted flow of water at all times, if the flow slows, we have errors and the efficacy of the heat pump disappears. The units measure the flow rate
themselves with an ultrasonic flow switch this black thing. On some units they are lose for the plumbers to fit, on others they are built into the unit.

We want to know the speed of the water in case of error, we

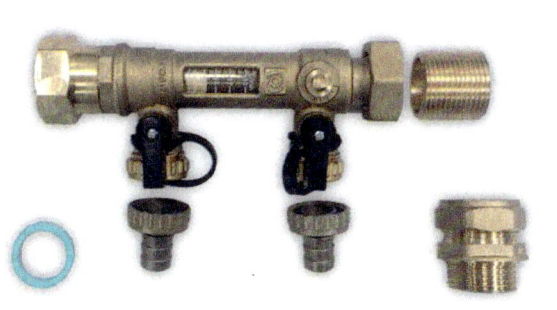

often also use a mechanical flow meter so its quick and easy to read. Manufacturers don't make reading the flow rate from the ultra-sonic meter as simple as they should, so the mechanical meter is there purely for convenience. We recommend a flow meter is installed in every system rated 0-40l/min

Robokit

If you buy an expansion vessel, safety valve, filling loop and gauge all together they call it a Robokit. The expansion vessel is there to absorb any expansion in the water as it heats and cools. Water does expand a bit as you heat it, his must be taken up in the system.

The expansion vessel is half full of air and half full of water, there is a bladder between the two to form a seal. As the water expands it pushes against the air.

There are different colour expansion vessels. Red or grey don't drink the water, white

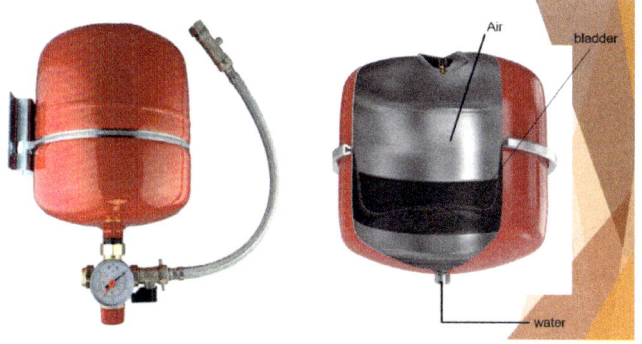

or blue ok to drink.

Low Loss header

The header is discussed in detail in a later question about flow rate. But its job is to separate the water flowing through

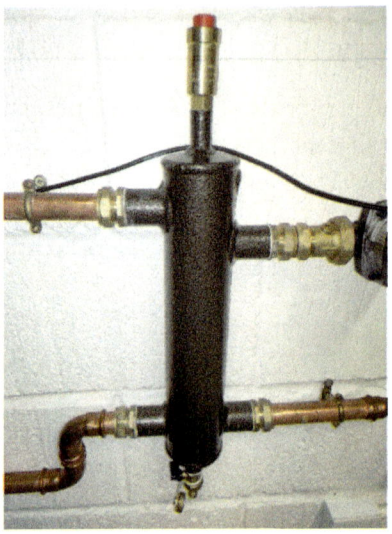

the heat pump and the radiators, there are often differences in speed in these two circuits, the header allows the water to flow separately. They are the size of a 2-litre coke bottle.

Heat exchanger

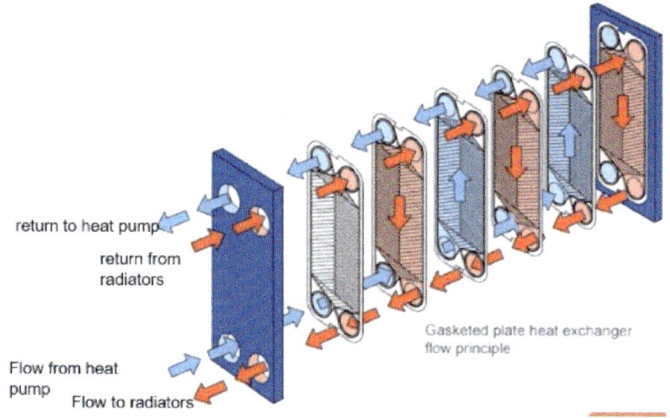

Gasketed plate heat exchanger flow principle

A heat exchanger does the same job as a low loss header, but the two streams of water don't actually mix, they come very close to each other but don't mix. See the blue flow is through the heat pump, it has antifreeze in it. The red flow is through the radiators it doesn't have anti-freeze in it.

Fused spur and Isolator

An isolator is a massive switch which is waterproof, there will be one on your heat pump outside. You turn the red knob to switch it on and off, so they call it a rotary isolator.

A fused spur is just a heavy-duty switch with a fuse in it, they fix to the wall with a metal or plastic box called a Patrice. It's used inside the house.

Electric meters

It is now a requirement to measure the electricity being used by the heat pump so the end user can see what the unit costs to run, although the unit can now estimate the energy used, we always recommend 2 smart electric meters are used. Ideally it should measure the total draw for the heat pump (outdoor and indoor unit combined). The outdoor unit takes most of the current so in many installations it will only be

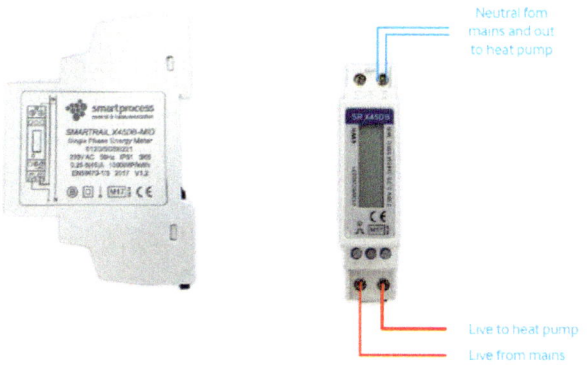

used to measure the outdoor unit.

Glycol / antifreeze

In Monobloc heat pumps the water goes outside the building. The unit can protect itself from freezing up, but if the power goes off there is a risk that the unit will freeze causing damage.

To prevent this, we recommend putting propylene glycol (food grade antifreeze) mixture in the system. It is important that the glycol concentration is adequate to protect the unit, if the unit freezes up there will be no warranty. Manufacturer dependant, a mix of 25% is normal for UK conditions.

Adding too much glycol is not a good idea, it increases the water pump power and slightly reduces the capacity of your system.

63 Under floor heating how it works

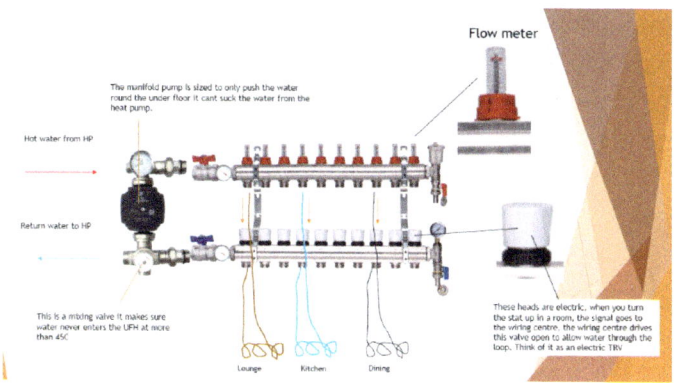

An underfloor heating system is simple. Instead of having radiators on the walls of the room the heating engineers lay a pipe, it's like having a hose pipe buried in the floor either in concrete called screed or in specially cut floors which hold the tubes in place. Basically, you are replacing the steel radiator with a long length of plastic pipe hidden away out of sight. It's obvious that in a normal sized room the size of the floor is much bigger than the average radiator so in effect you have a room sized concrete radiator.

Because its big it has the advantage, we don't need to run it as warm as a radiator. See q 8 and 9.

In most rooms you would have one loop of pipe per room, but if the room is very large it sometimes has 2 or even more loops under the floor. Each loop tends to be less than 200m long.

Each of the loops is connected back to a central point where the heating engineers install a manifold. This is basically a connection point to bring each of the loops back together wo make them easy to connect to your heat pump. Think of the manifold as a big connector block.

Control.

In every room you have a room thermostat, when you turn it up and ask for heat it sends a signal back to a wiring centre next to the manifold, this signal gets sent to an electric valve on the manifold which slowly opens and lets the water flow into the loop in the floor of that room.

In this way you can heat each room independently of each other. The valve on the manifold is basically an electric version of the white radiator valves we are all familiar with. On the better manifolds they also have tiny flow meters, they are basically tiny speedos showing how much water is going into each loop.

It's important that each room gets the right amount of water to heat it. It's not rocket science but the bigger the room the greater the amount of water the room needs. If all your underfloor loops are set to the same flow rate either you have a house where all the rooms are the same size, or it's been set up badly. The art of setting up the underfloor is called balancing. It's worth asking the installer for the underfloor design, on it will be the recommended flow rate.

A badly balanced underfloor heating system will ruin the heating performance of your system, it is very common.

64 Show all types of standard installations and what goes into them

I'm going to concentrate on a couple of Brands, but they are all very similar, all you need to know is does your heat pump have a pump inside or not.

Units with no pumps inside: Every Samsung Monoblock must have a control box called a MIM, it comes with a flow switch and remote controller and hot water tank sensor inside the box.

The Samsung Monoblock units need to have a pump, 2 x 2 port valves and hydraulic separator (buffer, plate, or low loss header) installed. We separate the radiator and UFH circuit from the flow through the heat pump as they operate at completely different flow rates.

The heating circuit connects after the header, you can do anything you like here, it's possible to have as many pumps, zones or valves as you like here, they don't affect the heat pump.

The Samsung unit also needs a filter a flow switch and a flow meter on the return.

Electrically you need an isolator for the outdoor unit, a fused switch for the indoor controls and electric meters to measure exactly what electricity you are using.

Units with pumps in them. Every

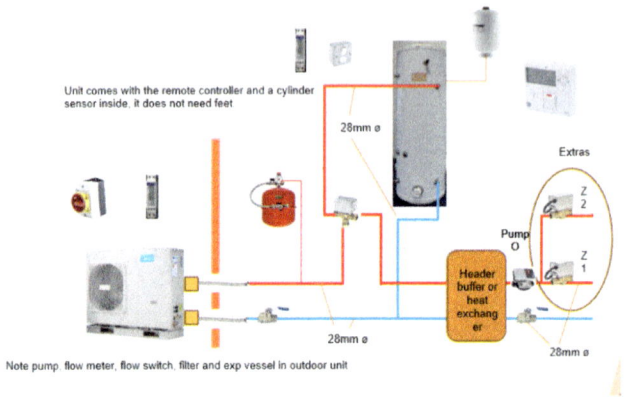

Midea Mono Heating and Hot Water Install pack

Midea Monoblock has the control box inside the unit, it comes with a flow switch installed. The remote controller and hot water tank sensor inside the box to be installed in the house.

The Midea Monoblock units have a pump inside, in the house we use a 3-port valve and hydraulic separator (buffer, plate or low loss header) installed. We must separate the radiator and UFH circuit from the flow through the heat pump as they operate at completely different flow rates.

The heating circuit connects after the header, you can do anything you like here, it's possible to have as many pumps, zones or valves as you like here, they don't affect the heat pump.

Electrically you need an isolator for the outdoor unit and an electric meter to measure exactly what electricity you are using.

65 What's a pre plumbed cylinder

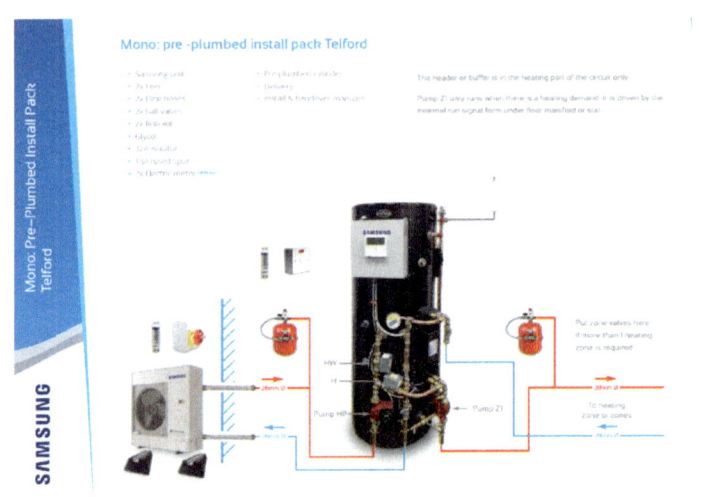

To Make life easier you can buy a pre- wired, pre-plumbed, pre-commissioned package. The lads in the factory bolt all the loose parts onto a cylinder and set it all up before it leaves. There are now Pre plumbed cylinders for all Samsung heat pumps.

Now your plumber and sparky fix the outdoor unit outside, put the tank on the floor, connect the interconnecting pipework between the outdoor unit and the tank, the radiators and the tank and the hot and cold feeds and wiring and flick the switch.

What's the drawback? it's a bit big, so getting it through a loft hatch can be a challenge.

Is it horribly expensive? No, its £500 more than buying a pile of boxes.

66 Minimum system volume

Many manufactures specify a minimum system volume in their system. Samsung ask for 50 litres of water in the system. They say this is to stop the units stopping and starting too much but its really to protect the unit from freezing up when its defrosting.

This has become a major issue in the last 2 years, some manufacturers are more instant than others

Midea do not have a minimum system volume. Daikin and Samsung are much more concerned the volume is correct.

A buffer vessel is just a big bucket with lots of connections on it. It simply holds a volume of water, it's the same water that flows through the heat pump and the radiators. To the untrained eye it looks very much like a hot water cylinder, but the difference is there is no coil inside. Think of it as a big, insulated bucket storing hot water.

Why do people use them?
In boiler land it's hard to run at low capacity, if you turn down the flame too much it goes out, so with a big Boiler a

buffer is used to improve efficiency and reduce number of start-ups per hour.

Your domestic boiler will probably give a maximum output of 20 or 30kW. Its minimum output will be something like 10kW. If you are only heating one room and only need 1kW your boiler will switch on and off as it provides too much heat for the output required.

If you use a buffer the boiler heats a few hundred litres of water to 70C and then stops.

The water from the buffer trickles through your one operating radiator and it might take 30 minutes or more before the buffer has dropped in temperature to 60C. At 60C the boiler starts again, heats the whole buffer back to 70C and the cycle repeats. This means the boiler runs flat out (when its most efficient) for short periods of time instead of

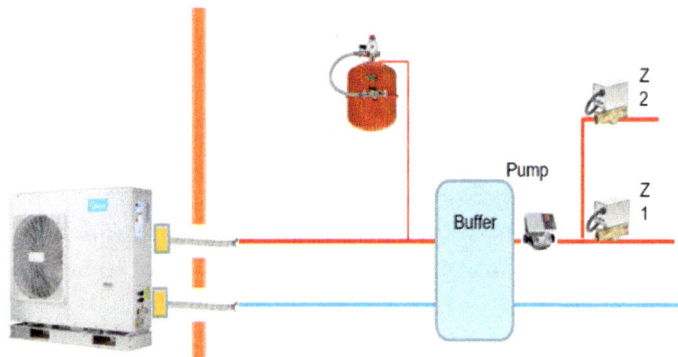

cycling on and off every few minutes.

When the first heat pumps came out, they were even worse than your boiler, they were fixed speed, so they were flat out 100% capacity or off, the had no capacity control so buffers were essential.

By 1990 inverters were widely available in air conditioning so all the big brands put them into heat pumps as they were developed. I've been in heat pumps for nearly 15 years, I have never sold a fixed speed heat pump. Until a couple of years ago this ancient technology was still available in heat pumps, it's embarrassing but old habits are hard to break. The old duffers tell you inverters are expensive and unreliable, every electric car is inverter driven, so is your vacuum cleaner if you bought it from Dyson.

Inverter driven heat pumps can turn down to about 10% of peak output to match the load of the house, this means even if you are only running one radiator the heat pump will trickle along matching the load, it doesn't need to cycle on and off, so the buffer is no longer required.

Some people love a buffer they use them because its traditional. I hate them, the problem is if you start the heating from cold you gave to heat the buffer too, so it slows down the heat up time, they also are full of hot water when the heating is finished which can be a waste. Oh, and they are big and expensive. Just one more reason not to buy a heat pump.

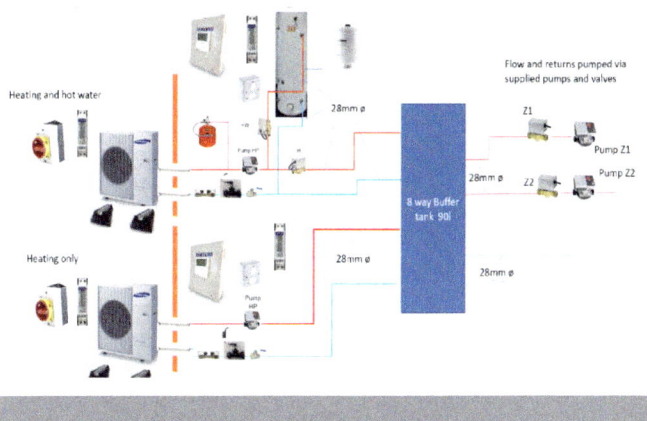

Buffers do have a couple of uses though, mostly in complex systems. We use them as a great way of combine multiple heat sources (see above) or if you want to use an aga, 2 or 3 heat pumps, a wood burner, solar thermal etc we connect them all into the big bucket. If you do this with some clever set up, you can use it to integrate multiple heat sources.

An average house uses 20 litres of hot water a minute to keep it hot in cold weather. That tank had the capacity to heat his house for an hour. Man was he ripped off. You can't store heat unless you have masses of volume and space, so don't bother. Just store it in the air outside and use it as you need it. That's what a proper inverter driven air source heat pump does.

67 Why is flow so important?

To work out flow rates you must do some heat maths using the specific heat capacity of water, 4.18kJ/kg/K or 4180W/litre/K

But it's easier to use rules of thumb:

A 70 Watts heater will lift one litre of water one degree C in one minute.

A 350-Watt heater will lift one litre by 5 C per minute

A 3500-Watt heater will lift ten litres of water by 5 C per minute

When we are measuring heat pump capacity, we often use this:

If the flow rate through the unit is 15 l/min every 1-degree temperature lift is 1kW

If the flow rate through the unit is 30 l/min every 1-degree temperature lift is 2kW

A heat pump is just a machine which adds 5 degrees C to water as it goes through, we call this a 5-degree Delta T. We must run our systems with a 5-degree delta T, this means flow at 50C, return at 45C, if we don't, we get horrible efficiencies.

We push the water through the pipes as fast as possible to get the best out of the units. The problem is if you push too fast the pipes become noisy. So, the rule is to never let the water move at more than 1.5 metres per second or 3 mph in

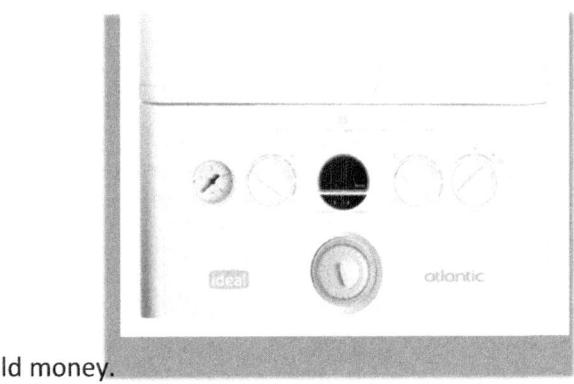

old money.

If we want to avoid noisy pipework, we can only push this many kWs through the pipes:

8mm pipe 1.2kW

10mm pipe 1.8kW

15mm pipe 4.5kW

22mm pipe 10kW

28mm pipe 16.8kW

There are only 3 things that matter in heat pumps, the first and most important thing is flow, once you have got that sorted next you need to concentrate on the flow and after that look at the flow again. Hilarious huh? but scarily true.

Heating engineers appear to find the whole idea of flow rate completely alien, it's something they have never had to bother with. In their defence its never been an issue so why learn it. Think about your house, all you care about is if the radiators are hot, you have no way to measure the flow rate to your heating and you don't care. If a room is not getting up to temperature you just wind up the boiler temperature using the very easy to operate controls and the increase in temperature means the rooms all get warm. see example below of superb and easy to use controls, see if you can work out how to turn up the boiler temperature?

In heat pumps flow is all that matters, we send out water at a lower temperature because the higher the temperature the more the heat pump costs to run, it's just like your car, faster is more expensive. You need to supply much more water to the radiators if the temperature is lower than you do if the water is really hot to keep the rooms warm. Typically, in a heat pump system we need to pump the water round at twice the speed as you do with a boiler.

What no one tells you is, if the flow rate falls below the optimum the efficiency of your heat pump falls dramatically, the output also falls and the run cost goes UP, UP, UP. If you have a heat pump you too should be obsessed with flow rate. You will never reach that published SCOP or efficiency figure if the flow rate is not high enough.

If you don't know what flow rate you need it's simple, take the unit model number and times by 2 and 2 ½, that's the range of how many litres per minute flow you need. Example: a 16kW unit needs a minimum of 32 litres a minute and a maximum of 40 litres a minute. If you have less flow than this, you are spending more money than you need too. Think of it as the equivalent of driving your car with the hand brake on a couple of notches.

This leaves us with a problem, if you want to move water down a pipe there is a speed range which works best, if you go too fast the water makes a hell of a noise, it sounds like a tap running, not ideal in a heating system. To get the speed down we increase the pipe size, very roughly as you increase the size from 15mm to 22m or 22mm to 28mm the speed of the water halves and the noise disappears, clever huh? that's why we use big pipes on heat pumps.

But the problem doesn't end there, you need bigger pumps and every bend, valve, fitting, filter etc in the pipe work slows the water down and creates a resistance. It's just like when you stand on a hose pipe when your wife/husband /kids are washing the car, hilarious and a good training in fluid flow and resistance.

Heat pumps usually have some way to detect how fast the water is moving, in the old days we used a paddle switch but now we use a flow meter like this.

Somewhere inside your unit you can see what this meter is reading. Think of this thing as your systems speedometer. BUT the heat pump manufacturers hide this data from you, it is without doubt the single most important piece of information you and the end user need to know about the unit, so the software guys hide it. I have no idea why they do this, but they all need a bloody good kicking, this info should

be displayed on the front screen all the time.

So we put a mechanical flow meter on all out heat pump packs like this, anyone can read it anytime.

68 Why do we use a header, a plate heat exchangers or buffer? what is hydraulic separation.

Novices (and shiny suited salesmen) think you can tube heat pumps up like this.

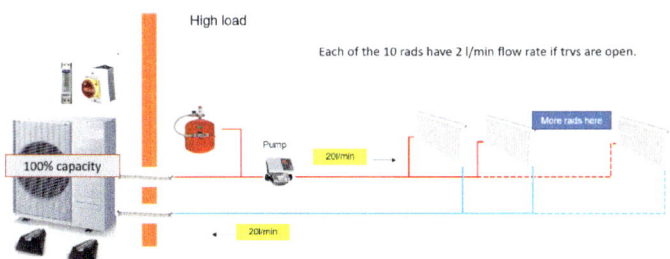

This works brilliantly if the TRV'S, those white valves on the end of your radiators, never close and the flow rate doesn't change, ever. This is a pipe dream.

The problem is that every heat pump I've ever seen has a flaw, the water flow rate cannot change no matter what the load is. We have massive, fixed speed pumps forcing the water round the system blissfully ignorant of what the actual load in the building is. It is, in my opinion a design error which started back 12 years ago and has never been addressed. When you are in a low load condition you get this issue:

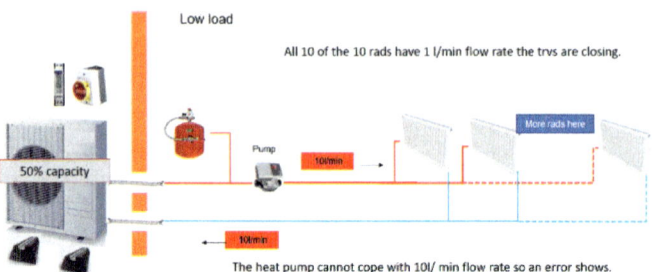

The flow slows down and the unit trips out on low flow alarm.

In the old days we solved this with a bypass, if the flow dropped the bypass opened to allow a short circuit to maintain flow rate. It was OK but the installers refused to set it up correctly, quite rightly they thought the unit would cope. They were wrong.

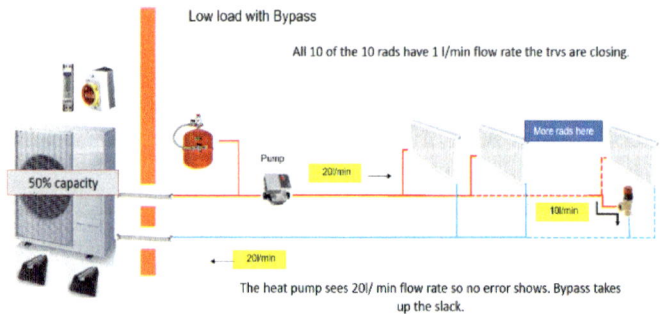

As tech support engineers we got fed up with this and decided to use a low loss header or plate heat exchanger to stop this problem, it's a good solution but it's expensive. This diagram shows a low loss in high load, at this point it's not doing anything, the flow in and out is balanced.

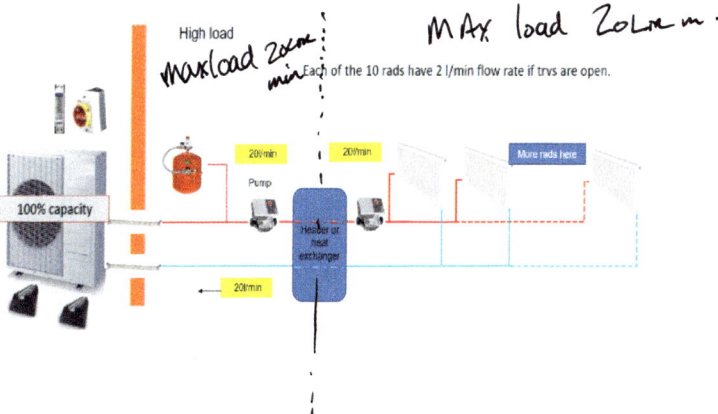

But when the load on the secondary (right hand side) side falls and the flow rate slows the low loss does its thing. As you can see here. the speed through the heat pump is

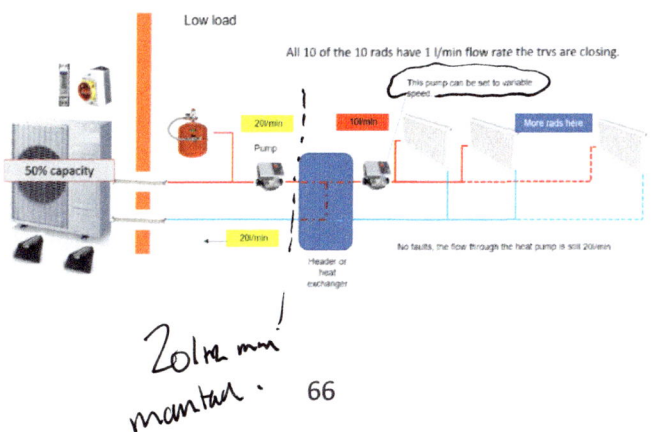

constant and the speed through the heating circuit falls, the header evens things out.

There are other more obtuse ways of doing this like the volumiser route below, this is favoured by plumbing geeks, but it's just the same as using a low loss header.

If the manufacturers would just allow the unit to have variable flow rate or link it to the compressor speed, we could do this and save hundreds of pounds in installation cost and save the run cost of 2 pumps.

It's a simple thing to do, the unit knows the water is moving as it measures the delta t (water temp difference) across the unit. If the delta is very high the water is moving slowly, if the delta is low the water must be moving quickly.

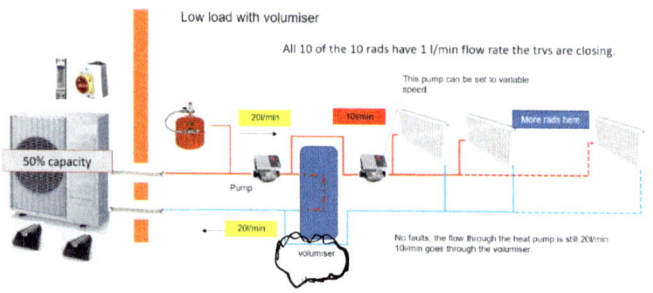

69 What's the difference between primary and secondary flow

Primary flow is the water that goes through the heat pump, its described below:

Getting the water to move around the heat pump is easy, most of the pipework will be new and if your heat pump

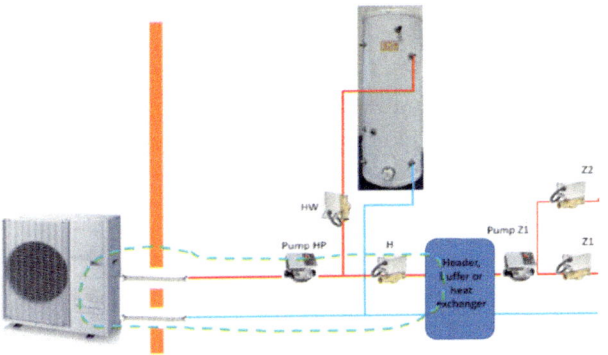

designer is good, it will be the right size.

The water flow shown in green here will go through the heat pump and the efficiency should be pretty good, remember the rule: take the kW of the heat pump and make the flow rate 2- 2.5 X that figure, so 16kW unit needs 32 - 40 l/min.

In hot water mode we move the valves around and force the water through the cylinder. Again, if it's well designed and installed you should get amazing flow rates and efficiencies. But be careful, if you use a cylinder with a coil smaller than 3m^2, they sing when the water is flowing through them, it's

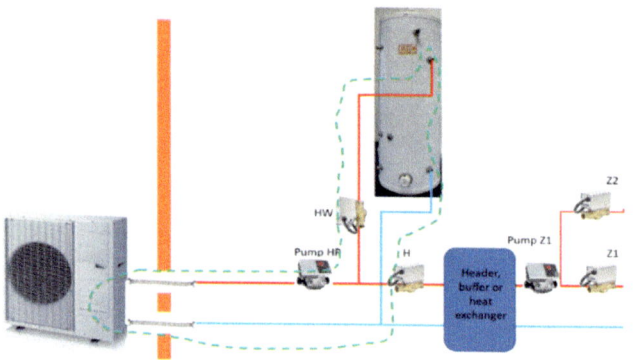

like a low bass rumble, it's annoying. If this happens you need to slow the water in hot water mode, to avoid the homeowner going bezerk. Some heat pumps have this provision and speed control built in, most don't.

The primary flow is all your heat pump manufacturer is worried about. The secondary flow rate (in green below) is the flow rate after the header buffer or plate heat exchanger. See q 66 this is only in the circuit to stop the units tripping in low load conditions.

This secondary flow is extremely important, but almost no

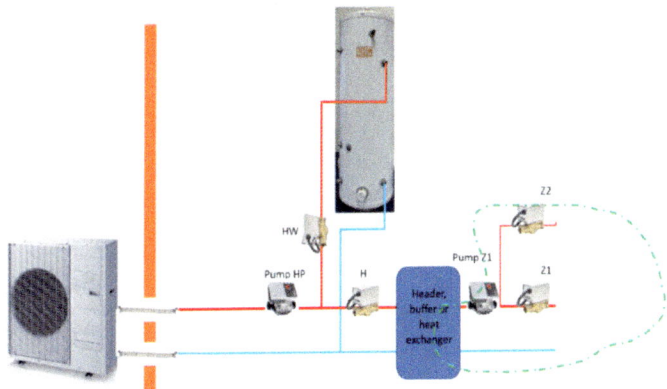

heat pump on the market measures it, they simply have no idea what's going on out in the system. Some don't even have the provision to control the secondary pump, (pump z1 in the drawing) so it's possible that the heat pump can be

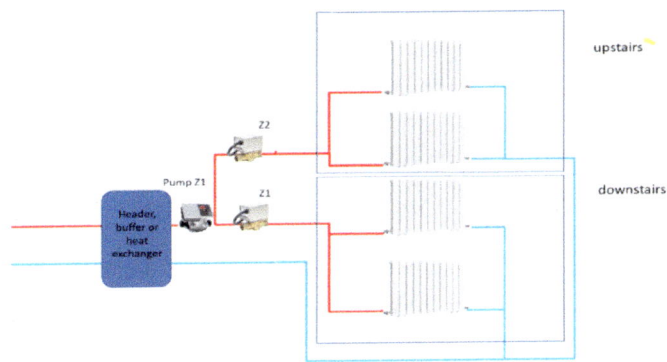

operating with no secondary flow at all. Everything's getting hot but none of the hot water is reaching the radiators.

Your system at home is piped up like this, the radiators are all in parallel with each other, if you have a big house, it's probably split into 2 zones or more.

It doesn't take a genius to work out that if only 1 zone is running, let's say only valve Z1 is open, the flow rate in the secondary circuit is not as fast as if both zones are operating. In an ideal world the heat pump will react to this and adjust its output and flow rate to suit.

In a good system, the plumber will adjust the flow rate to each radiator so it's just right to maintain the room temperatures in the house, (if the flow is too high the rooms roast and if it's too low the room is cold). If it's balanced like this, then all the rooms reach temperature at roughly the same time. If you have thermostatic radiator valves on your system, you can badly control the room temperatures in the house by twiddling the knob on the radiator and the plumber doesn't have to balance the radiators. But here is the rub, imagine a warm day, the rooms get to temperature and the radiator valves close, so the flow rate slows down in the secondary circuit. it's possible you could be heating just one or two radiators and remember, no one tells the heat pump what's going on.

In my system I have a total of 150 litres of water in all the pipes and radiators, the primary circuit only holds about 25 litres the rest is in the secondary. So, if I was to run only the primary circuit the unit could overheat or worse, freeze up in defrost mode. Some manufacturers are paranoid about this, it's because they can't reliably access the water in the secondary circuit. If your heat pump manufacturer makes you put a volumiser or buffer in the primary circuit so they have access to the minimum volume of water which could be used for defrosting, you know they have no control over secondary flow.

My advice if you have one of these systems is to remove all the zone valves after the header and put lock shield, tamperproof radiator valves on every rad in the house, I will also arrange for the secondary pump to run all the time the primary pump is running in heating mode. That way you have loads of system volume and loads of secondary flow rate. No buffer or volumiser is required. You have just engineered a solution that the heat pump designer and manufacturer couldn't be bothered to do.

The clever thing to do would have a system where the heat pump knew exactly what is going on in the secondary part of the circuit by measuring the temperatures. That way it could see that the zones were closing and adjust the output of the heat pump to match.

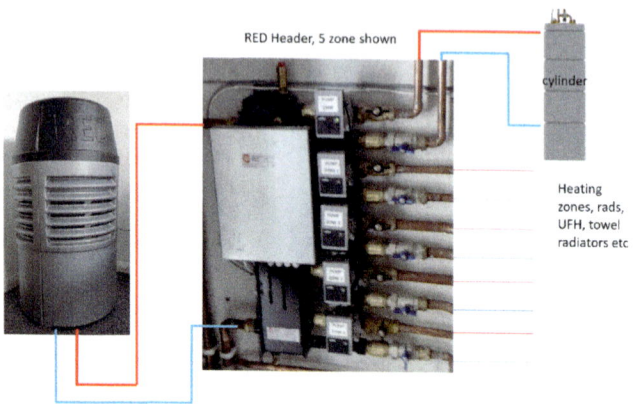

But these features are very, very rare indeed. I only know of one unit that does this, our RED system. It is in complete control of the flow on both side of the system and works to balance these all the time. It manages the secondary flow rate to maintain a constant temperature difference across each zone and in defrost all the pumps run (except in hot water mode). It means you get the best from your system all the time. It's expensive but very clever. Simplicity is very hard to achieve.

70 What happens if the flow is too slow or too fast?

Too slow and you can't deliver the heat to the house quickly enough and you get flow errors and poor efficiency.

Too fast and you get noise in the system and pipework, and you spend extra on pumps, pipes, and energy to move the water.

I have very rarely seen too fast flow.

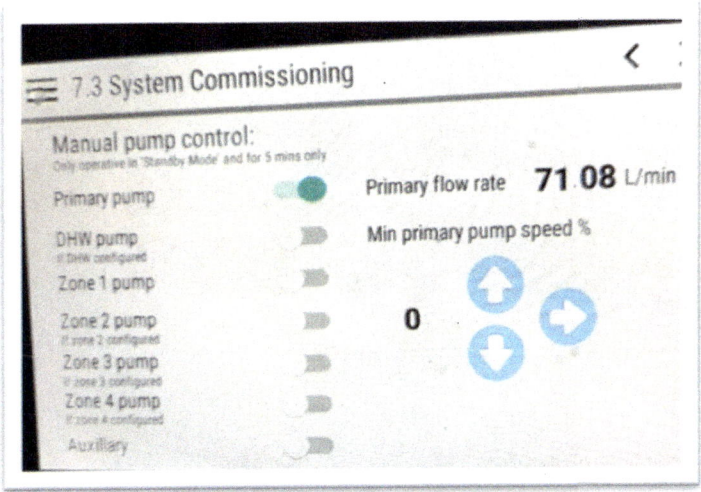

71 What's a PWM pump

Standard pumps have only one cable, the heat pump can only switch this on or off, it cannot adjust its speed. They are dumb. They often have speed control knobs or buttons on the front, this one has an arrow button.

Note there is often a socket for a second cable but its not used.

Pulse Width Modulation. (allows speed control of the pump by an external control).

PWM pumps are more sophisticated than standard pumps.

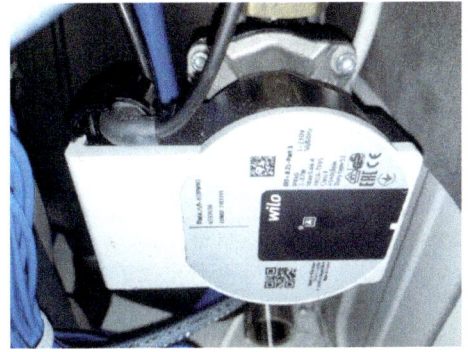

They have 2 cables connected to them, one provides power, and the other is the speed controller. These pumps are controlled by the heat pump itself. Look for two sperate cables into the pump like this.

PWM pumps are more expensive to buy, they used to be very expensive, so we didn't use them but now they are only about 20% more so they are becoming more popular. If the speed cable is disconnected, they run flat out all the time.

Because PWM pumps are more sophisticated some manufacturers can tell the flow rate through the pump with the second lead. This means we don't need an extra flow meter.

72 Thermal stores and heat pumps

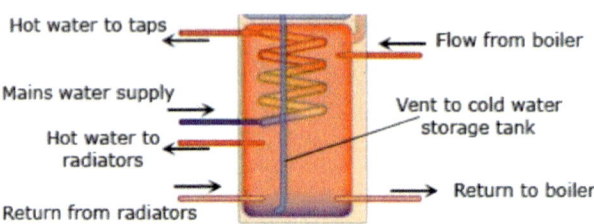

A thermal store is like a buffer vessel and a hot water cylinder all in one, imagine a hot water cylinder but with loads of connections on the side.

It's a big bucket filled with the water, the water inside the store is not the water you bathe in its the water that goes through the boiler. It's just like a buffer, but it also has a coil running through it to make instant hot water for your taps. Cold water enters the coil and is heated instantly by the water in the bucket, it leaves as hot water which goes to your taps.

The beauty of a store is you can use wood burners, solar panels boilers etc all connected together to heat the house and hot water. Heating consultants like me call this integrating the technologies together. The only problem is stores are horrible when you use them on heat pumps, let me explain.

The thermal store needs to be kept very hot so you can make instant hot water as described above. Typically, they are kept between 60 and 70C all the time even in summer, you never know when the homeowner will want a shower. Boilers are brilliant at this, so a store looks like a good idea. But in heat pump land we want to run the water to the radiators and underfloor heating at a lower temperature to make the run cost low and run at a high temperature to heat the hot water cylinder. Running a heat pump all year round at high temperatures is never going to be efficient or cheap.

Most people want access to hot water pretty much 24/7. We want to go to the hot tap turn it on and hot water comes out. If your hot water is provided by a thermal store that means you must keep the whole store hot all the time and it has to be the same temperature all year round. Why is this so bad? We keep the hot water cylinder hot all year. In a store the hot water and the heating all come from the same place, but typically in a UK house you use 5-10 times as much energy to heat the house as you do the hot water so keeping the heating super-hot just so you can have a hot shower is wasteful.

Heat pumps are most efficient when running at low temperatures, the hotter the water they supply the more it costs, it's just the way it is, no one can do anything about it. So, to get the most efficient operation the key is to run the heat pump at lower temperatures in heating mode and high temperatures in hot water mode.

In a store you can't weather compensate, it must be as hot as possible all the time so it can provide hot water. The hotter the water in the store the more water you can have, the worst bit about stores is you just don't get much hot water unless it's very hot, example: If we hold a 300L store at 55C, you only get 80 litres of water out of it at before it drops to 45C, then the store temperature is too cold and the water coming out the taps starts to drop in temperature. So, you have a massive tank but not much hot water.

In conclusion: Don't use thermal store on a heat pump. If you have one its amazing either rip it out and sell it on eBay or leave it just in the heating part of the circuit to combine other heating source to the heat pump and put in a new heat pump cylinder for your hot water.

I get asked about stores at least every couple of weeks, "can I keep my thermal store" NO.

73 What is a monobloc? The boiler in the Garden.

A monobloc heat pump is basically a heat pump designed to replace your boiler all mounted in one The installer will disconnect the boiler and extend the pipes out to the unit in the garden.

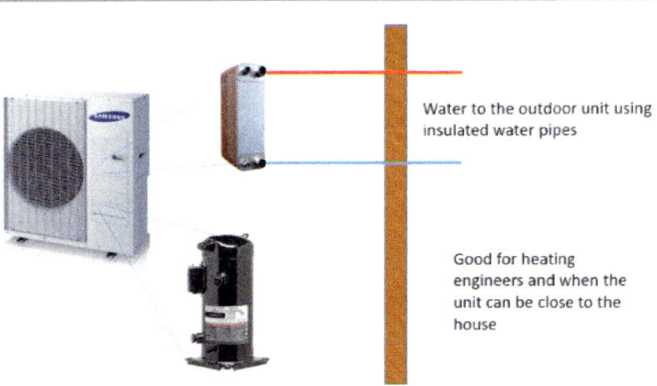

Water to the outdoor unit using insulated water pipes

Good for heating engineers and when the unit can be close to the house

Because we have to extend the water pipework out to the unit in the garden, It costs more to connect the unit a long way from the house. It's hard to pump water long distances. Typically, if the unit needs to go a long way from the house, we avoid this type of system purely because its costly. As a rule if the heat pump is less than 15m from the hot water cylinder a monobloc is a good idea, further than that we opt for a split system.

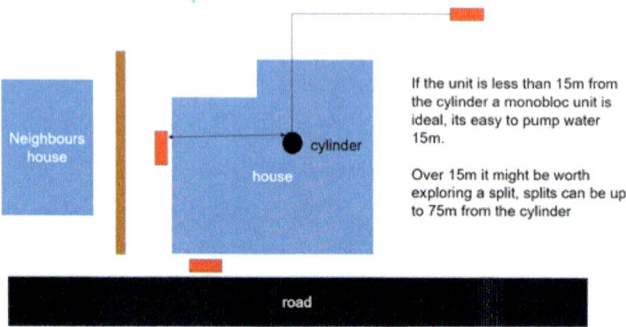

use split systems. We will discuss this later.

Advantages of monos: They are simple, you don't need a fridge (fgas) engineer, if they go wrong, they are easy to change, there is very little kit needed inside the house, most components are in the unit in the garden, so they save space.

With the new more flammable refrigerants it's a good idea to keep them outside the house.

Disadvantages with monos: the water goes outside so you need bigger pumps to push and pull it around the system, the water could freeze so they must put anti-freeze in.

Its expensive to put these along way from the house.

74 What is a split? - the unit comes in 2 pieces with the boiler indoors.

If you want to put the heat pump well away from the house its often a good idea to use a split system.

A split is simply a monobloc unit cut into two pieces. They connect together using much smaller refrigerant pipe work so they are amazing when you want to go for a long pipe run,

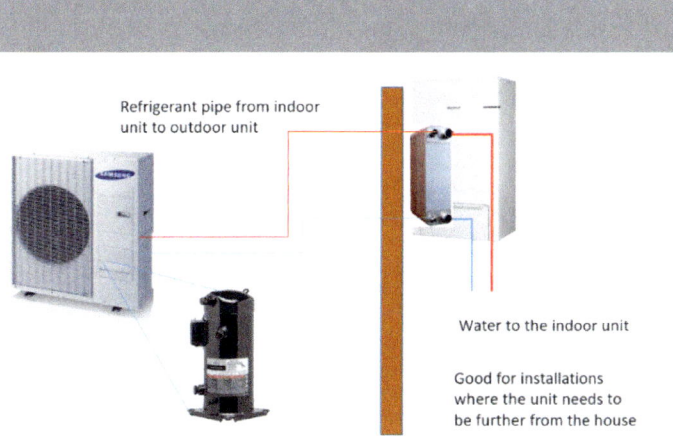

Refrigerant pipe from indoor unit to outdoor unit

Water to the indoor unit

Good for installations where the unit needs to be further from the house

most splits can be up to 75 m apart.

In a split system, the unit is cut in half, you have a unit outside and a box like a boiler inside. The water pipes to the boiler unit (hydro box). The two boxes are separated by fridge pipework. The box outside houses the compressor and coil, the indoor box houses a pump and a heat exchanger

Advantages of splits: the water does not go outside so you need smaller pumps to push and pull it around the system and you don't need anti-freeze. They can go 75m down the garden using tiny pipework. It's cheaper to put these along way from the house.

Disadvantages with split: You need a fridge (fgas) engineer, if they go wrong, they are harder to change, the unit inside is boiler sized so you must put it somewhere. Hitachi now do a split system where the indoor unit and the cylinder are all in one box called the Combi.

With modern refrigerants its often difficult to meet the regulations to install any refrigerant In the house.

75 What's FGAS?

FGAS is a qualification a bit like gas safe.

FGAS engineers have been trained to make sure that none of the refrigerants in the system leak into the atmosphere.

It is illegal to work on refrigerant systems if you don't have an FGAS certificate.

Monoblock units are like fridges, they are sealed up so anyone can work on them.

Split systems need an fgas engineer to work on the system as it is built on site and must be filled with FGAS.

76 Can I heat the water to 50C with a heat pump and boost it to 70C with a boiler

Consultants often come up with a great idea for big house. They design a system with a heat pump and a boiler or backup heater like the systems we talked about in Q28.

But they come up with an interesting idea, why not use the heat pump to warm the water up to 50C and let the boiler

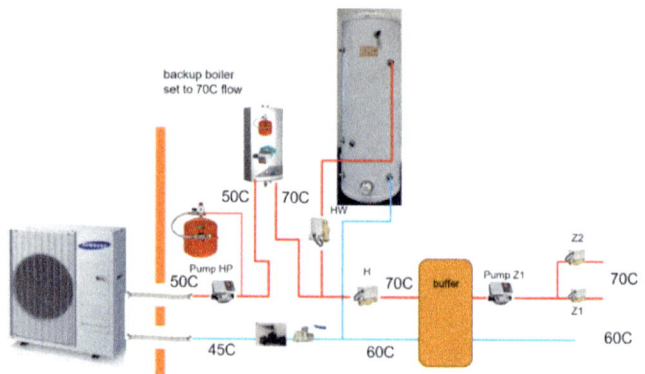

raise it to 70C. The problem is it doesn't work.

If you look at the diagram above, it all looks ok to begin with but…. the water comes into the heat pump at 45C, it leaves at 50C. It goes into the boiler which raises it to 70C.

The water trundles off to the radiators at 70C and comes back at 60C where it arrives at the heat pump. Apart from causing over temperature errors because the heat pump cant handle this temperature there is nothing for the heat pump to do. Its set to send water out at 50C but the water is already hotter than that. It looks like the boiler will do all the work.

The only solution to this is in Q28 hybrids and backups.

77 do I need a plant room?

Heat pumps are designed to go outside, they are weatherproof.

Should pumps, controls, cylinders etc go outside? Obviously not, they are electrical components and need to be weather proofed.

To house all the pipes wires, pumps headers etc we need a space.

We need to allow 600mm x 600mm for the cylinder

We need to allow 850 x 600 for a pre plumbed cylinder.

This photo shows an ideal plant layout in a loft. It makes it easier to install if there is space. Its possible to scrunch everything up but it can look untidy.

78 Can a heat pump go on the wall or roof?

We prefer the units to be floor mounted, it makes installation, servicing, and replacement easier.

If they must be mounted on the wall, try to keep them low down out of sight especially from neighbours. They are hung on the wall with wall brackets like this.

Think about vibration, any noise from the unit will go into the brickwork

If the unit goes on the roof, it needs extra sound deadening. Most people put a polystyrene slab under a concrete slab, then put the unit on top on flexi feet to avoid noise drumming through the roof. There are custom mounting kits available for rooves like the one below.

The biggest challenge is getting the unit up onto the roof or brackets, they are over 100kG so lifting gear like this genie lift are needed.

Think: how are you going to lift the unit onto the roof or the brackets?

79 If I live by the sea will my unit rust?

Your heat pump sits outside the house in all weathers, sun, rain, and snow. If you don't look after them eventually, they fade and start to look tired and unloved, just like you would if you laid out in the weather all day without a bit of moisturiser. If you live by the sea like I do, in Southampton it's even worse.

Eventually the sea air and spray will rust the metalwork of the unit, despite the claims of the manufacturers, who all treat their coils with special coatings, the tin work is going to

rust.

In Saline conditions you need to have your unit coated with Bronzglow or Blygold, they are like varnishes which protect the paintwork. Some manufacturers do this for you as an option and call the units coastal. But if you forget, or you are in a rush to install, or the installer drills holes in the unit to put the cables in, it ruins the paint coatings. The units rust.

I advise everyone sprays every unit with ACF50 once a year no matter where its installed, ACF50 is like pink olive oil, you spray it on and wipe it over the unit with a rag. It comes up shiny. You can use it on metal or plastic, and it looks amazing.

Nothing ever rusts with ACF50 on it. It lasts about a year then you do it again.

80 If I mount the heat pump on a South facing wall, does it work better?

Every day we get asked if it makes any sense to install your heat pump in the sunshine. It's a common myth because it's in the sun it will be more efficient. Heat pumps have higher efficiencies in warmer weather than cold, so putting them in the sunshine must help right?

Heat pumps generally want to know the temperature of the air coming in. They need this information to control defrost, fan speeds and load calculations to control compressor speed and valve positions. It's important to the unit that its correct.

So, I thought I would test it out, I quickly assembled a rig using one of our exhibition units, I, taped on some cardboard side panels on to stop the wind and placed the unit in direct sunlight. With the unit switched off within a few minutes the temperature in the box was 25 C. The air temperature measured in the shade was 20 C. The temperature down the back of the unit was 23 C and rising. Therefore, people think this makes the efficiency better in sunlight, the temperature down the back of the unit is warmer so efficiency is better, obviously. BUT....... as soon as the fan starts up the temperature in the box and down the back of the unit falls to the real air temperature of 20 C. A heat pump like the one in the picture moves 50 m^3 of air every minute. If the unit had been in the shade all along the air temperature going through the unit would be the same.

A 16kW unit moves 100 m^3 of air every minute.

A 40-foot container is 12m*2.35m*2.4m that's 68 m^3

your heat pump moves a container worth of air every 40 seconds.

The major heat pump manufacturers worked this out years ago. If you watch your heat pump closely it spins the fan for a few seconds before the compressor starts, it is doing this to get rid of any standing air so it can measure the real air temperature. By simply putting a sensor on the back of the unit by the coil and spinning the fans for a few seconds they avoid having to have a remotely mounted air sensor, its simple, cheap, and effective.

So should we mount the unit in the sun? simply put the answer is put it wherever you like. But bear this in mind. Most units have a function where the unit wont heat above a pre-set air temperature to stop them running all summer long. It should be set to something like 21 C (why are you heating the house if its 21 C outside?) and mount the unit in direct sunlight it won't start up on cold, still days in the full sun. Its a problem we see at about this time of year on some old units.

81 Can I have more than one cylinder with a heat pump?

Most heat pumps come with the ability to heat a single hot water cylinder. They only come with one temperature sensor.

To heat more than one cylinder with a single heat pump poses us designers with a challenge.

If you can avoid it, I suggest you do.

If the cylinders are very close to each other there are some solutions to kid the unit, it only has one cylinder. If they are more than a metre or two apart, I don't recommend any of these solutions.

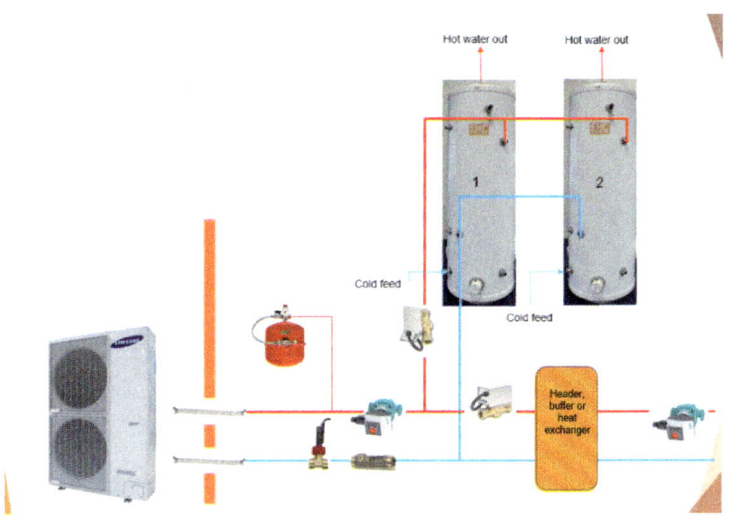

How NOT to do it:

In this example the plumber has just tubed 2 cylinders together. Water is lazy, it wants to take the shortest path, more water is going to go from the heat pump through the coil in cylinder 1 than cylinder 2 because its les distance, so the 2 cylinders won't be at the same temperature.

Also note that the hot water will drain to the taps easier from tank 1, its closer. Less water will leave cylinder 2, this system is not balanced properly.

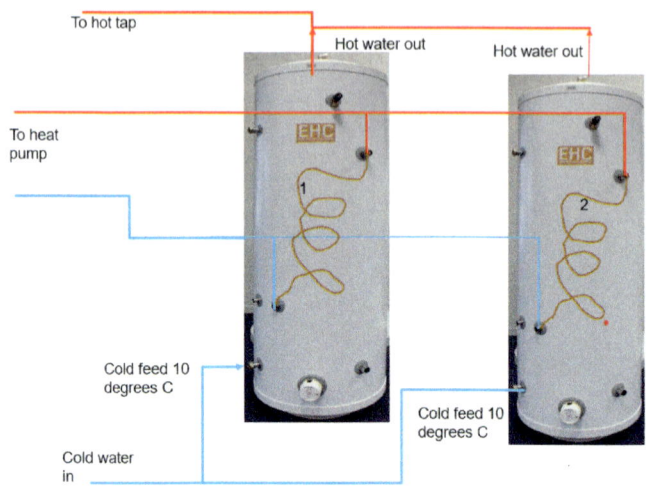

The solution is to make the resistance through the system perfectly balanced, so the water wants to flow through both cylinders at the same speed. We do this by using the same length pipework to both cylinders, it is called reverse return. It looks weird but it's done to balance out the flow.

Note how the flow into tank 1 is short but the return is long, it's the opposite on tank 2. We do the same on the cold feed

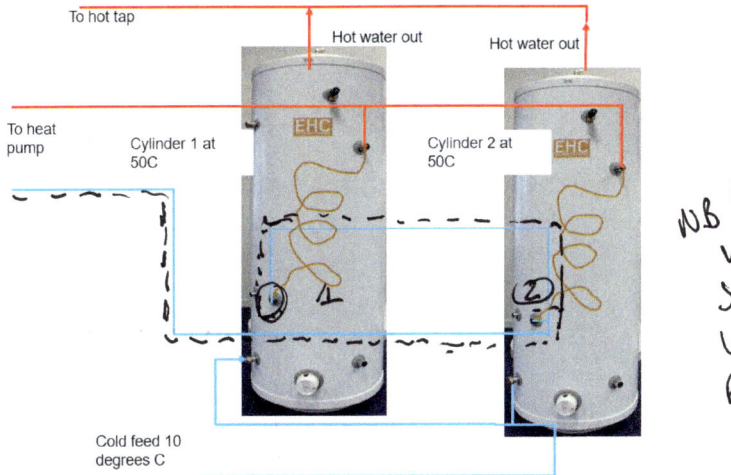

and the hot out of the tank. If we pipe the cylinders up so the total length of pipe to each cylinder is the same, the water will want to flow through each one at the same speed. Note how the flow pipe from the heat pump is short, but the return pipe is longer on cylinder 1.

82 An alternative, Using 2 Cylinders in Series

In this configuration we send the hottest water from the heat pump through the coil in cylinder one, then send it through the coil in cylinder 2. Cylinder 1 is hot at 50C, but cylinder 2 is much colder, it's like a pre-heater. The advantage is this is easy to tube up, but the disadvantage is we don't know the temperature of cylinder 2, it could be full of cold water.

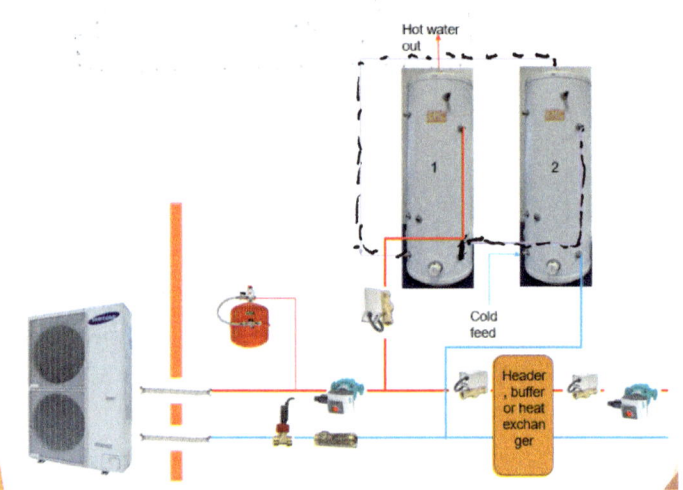

83 Can the cylinder go in the loft? Can it be horizontal? And can it go outside?

Cylinders are not waterproof; they need to go inside a building. They need to be protected from frost.

Most cylinders lose 1 kWhr of heat per day if they are in the house, if they are in the cold, they will lose twice this amount.

A 300L cylinder holds 13.5 kWhrs of heat. The heat from the cylinder leaks into the house so it's not a total waste but if its

outside it leaks away giving no benefit.

Putting the cylinder on the patio like this is not a good idea.

Putting it in a shed insulated with Celotex 25mm thick like this is very popular and a brilliant idea. Its like a mini plant

room.

Some people put the cylinder in the loft, there are custom horizontal heat pump cylinders to do this, but check the loft hatch size, cylinders tend to be 600mm diameter.

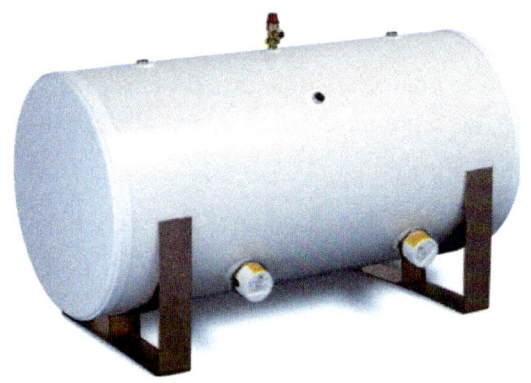

84 If I have 3 flats, can I serve them with one heat pump and a single cylinder?

It is possible to heat more than one property with a single heat pump, it's a popular idea in small flats, but there are a few things to consider.

If you have a system like this below, how do you know how much heat each flat has used so you can bill accordingly.

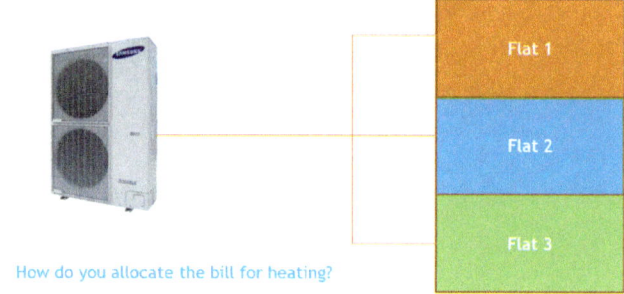

How do you allocate the bill for heating?

A few years ago we used to put simple meters on each flat and bill for what each flat used but nowadays you have to meter more accurately. You need to buy a heat interface unit. A heat interface unit is basically a metering unit the size of a combi boiler which measures how much heat goes into the flat. The problem is heat interface units cost £1000 Plus so they tend to kill the job off.

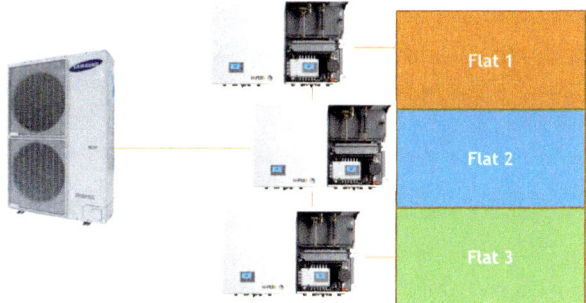
HIU or heat interface units (metering)

The next thing to consider is hot water. If you share a hot water cylinder between flats you need to measure who uses the water and how much they use. The heat interface unit will do this too.

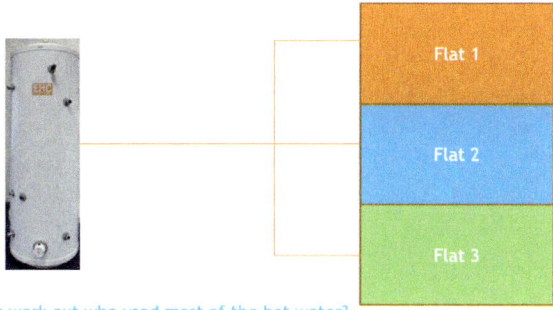
How do you work out who used most of the hot water?
What happens if the neighbour has a massive bath?

It can also be a challenge if one neighbour uses lots of hot water leaving you with a cold bath. These District heating systems are popular in flats where lots of buildings are served by a massive heating system, think hotel. The bigger the system the more sense it makes. But a big system will use a huge commercial heat pump, not a domestic unit like the ones we are used to.

85 Do I need a backup heater or immersion heater?

In Europe and Scandinavia, it's not uncommon for the heat pump to have a built in or factory supplied electric backup heater. The idea being that in extreme weather conditions the heat pump might need a bit of help so the electric heater can be bought in to help.

In the UK we don't do this. The golden rule in MCS is we must supply a heat pump which can heat the house which is big enough to heat the house to the design conditions (usually a room temperature of 21C) at the design ambient temperature listed here.

Below I have screen grabbed the rules from MCS, but in brief: electric backup heaters are allowed but we can't use them

Location	Altitude (m)	Hourly dry-bulb temperature (°C) equal to or exceeded for % of the hours in a year	
		A (99%)	B (99.6%)
Belfast	68	-1.5	-3.2
Birmingham	96	-3.2	-5.1
Cardiff	67	-1.5	-3.1
Edinburgh	35	-3.2	-5.4
Glasgow	5	-3.5	-5.9
London	25	-1.7	-3.0
Manchester	75	-2.7	-4.5
Plymouth	27	-0.2	-1.5

Table 2. Outside design temperatures for different locations in the UK taken from CIBSE Guide A Table 2.5, which also gives information on how to adapt and use this data.

until the ambient temperature falls below the design condition in column A here.

Bear in mind in an Average year the temperature only falls below this temperature for 72 hours a year.

If your heat pump has been designed properly the electric backup should not be required and would very rarely come on. When you have a boiler, it is also designed to run in these

5.5 SPACE HEATING DESIGN

5.5.1 For systems delivering space heating, the following procedure shall be followed for the correct sizing and selection of a heat pump and related components for each installation.

a) A heat loss calculation should be performed on the building using internal temperatures not less than those specified in Table 1 and external temperatures

e) A heat pump should be selected that will provide at least 100% of the calculated heat loss taking into consideration the flow temperature at the heat pump and without input from any supplementary electric heater. Performance data from both the heat pump manufacturer and the emitter system designer should be provided to support the heat pump selection.

conditions, but no one uses a backup heater for a gas boiler, heat pumps should be no different.

To prevent any risk of Legionella we heat the cylinder to 60C once a week, the heat pump heats the water to 50c, the immersion lifts it to 60C, it costs £1 a week to do this (33p/kWhr)

86 How hot is the hot water? will I need to boost it with a heater? what are you doing about legionella?

In most heat pump applications, we only heat the cylinder to 50 degrees C. The system will start heating the cylinder when it falls to 45C and stop heating it at 50 or 52C.

The water should come out of the taps at the same temperature as the water in the cylinder.

How hot is your shower? Or Bath?

A bath is usually 30-35C, any hotter and you can't get in. Showers are usually limited to 38C, you must press a button to get the water to come out hotter. At 50C you would not be able to get in the shower.

With a boiler the water often comes out hotter than 50C, we use a shower mixer or the cold tap to mix a bit of cold in to make it useable, it would be wasteful to do this with a heat pump.

To prevent any risk of Legionella we heat the cylinder to 60C once a week, we do this with an immersion heater it costs £1 a week to do this (33p/kWhr)

87 What's a secondary return pump / Hot water re-circulation pump?

In my job as tech support engineer one of the most common questions I get is how do I keep my run costs down on my heat pump? My first piece of advice is if you have a hot water re-circulation pump, cut the cable. Job done. These things can and will increase your electricity bill by hundreds of pounds a year.

Heat pumps cannot heat water instantly, they have inbuilt time delays and not enough capacity to heat water instantaneously, so we always use domestic hot water cylinders with this technology. Anyone who lives in a big house knows that it can take quite a while for the hot water to make it to the taps from the hot water cylinder. The accepted solution for this problem is to put a hot water ring main all around the house and a pump on it. The pump takes

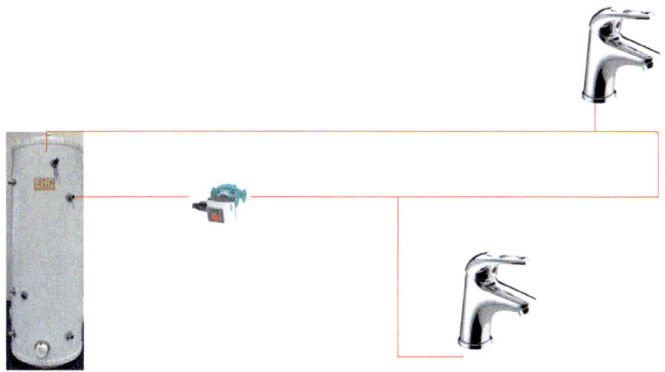

water from the cylinder and pushes it round the house so it's much closer to the taps. When you turn on the hot water tap out comes lovely warm water.

You can tell if you have this system because next to your cylinder there will be a re-circulation pump like this. They are usually orange. You will also probably be paying a fortune to heat your house and hot water.

Re-circulation pumps are a really good solution, but in almost every case its badly applied. let me explain.

The hot water loop is usually copper pipe, it is very rarely insulated (it should be) this acts as a radiator, slowly heating the house. The hot water comes back to the cylinder a bit and in some cases much colder. In time the cylinder temperature falls and the boiler or in my case the heat pump has to re heat it. So, if there is no re circulation pump, we might have to do 1 or 2 hot water cycles a day, but with a re circulation pump fitted it could be we have to do 10 or more cycles. In winter this is not so bad as the heating would be on anyway, but in spring, summer, and winter it's just burning money.

Engineers usually set them up so the pump is on 24 hours a day, it's not our money and we don't want you ringing us up saying that it took ages for the hot water to come out of the shower. run it 24/7 and you and the end user are happy until you see the bill.

But the sensible thing to do would be get the pump to run for the smallest possible period, literally a few minutes a day. Ideally the pump should start a few minutes before you jump in the shower and stop as soon as you are finished, it should not be running all the time you are at work and all the time you are asleep.

Some engineers will put a crude time clock on them, this is equally poor unless your hot water use is always the same, and check if you have a timer, we engineers tend to run them from 5 am till 12 pm so you don't call us. A while ago the big pump manufacturers started making these pumps with some intelligence, they learn your hot water usage and only operate to support that usage. These are an amazing idea. they retail for less than 200 quid, fit in place of the standard pumps, and will save their own cost in a matter of months.

And then the triple whammy, with a heat pump we use immersion heaters to help us if the heat pump is taking too long to heat the cylinder. In normal applications the immersion is rarely used except for the legionella cycle, but with a re circulation pump the hot water demand is massive and the unit is constantly struggling to keep up. So, you are actually heating the tank with an immersion, which in turn is heating the re circulation loop, which is heating the house. all by direct electricity.

So, your average hot water bill has now risen from £200 a year to 3,4 or 5 hundred pounds a year, and then you ring me, or you reach for those wire cutters.

88 Do I have to change every radiator? can I move some radiators around? can I keep my rads and suck it and see?

We discussed in q8 and 9 about radiators.

Most radiators in a conventional boiler installation will need water at 70C, if we provide water at 50C the radiator output will fall, this could leave you cold. We calculate this as part of the MCS heat load calculation and advise which radiators can be re used, moved, or replaced.

You very rarely have to replace every radiator; you do not need special radiators and you can move radiators from one room to another if you want too.

But the homeowner can choose to ignore this advice and not change the radiators. It just must be noted in the MCS heat loss. Once they have established which areas if any need a new radiator this can be replaced later.

We encourage the homeowner to run the heat pump 24/7 gently supplying heat to the room all the time, in a boiler its more likely to run for a few hours a day but at high temperature to raise the room temperature quickly. Slow and gentle and quick and aggressive still puts the same amount of heat into the room.

89 Can a heat pump re-use the pipework in my house, or will I have to have all of it changed?

In Q 67 we discussed flow rate.

We established we could comfortably push the following heat through the pipes without them getting too noisy.

8mm pipe 1.2kW

10mm pipe 1.8kW

15mm pipe 4.5kW

22mm pipe 10kW

28mm pipe 16.8kW down each pipe.

In the example installation above we will do the radiator sizing, all you have to do is work out how much heat is to go

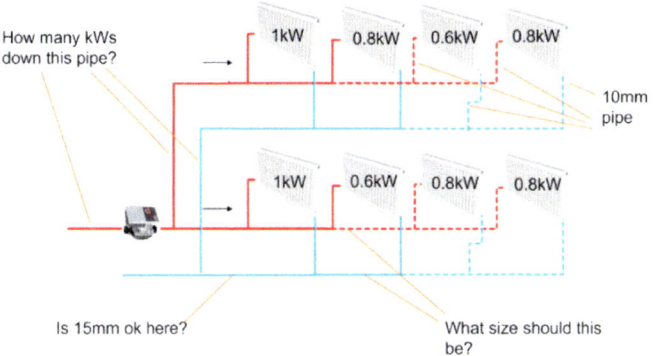

down each pipe.

Starting top right, the 0.8kW radiator needs a pipe of 8 mm or bigger, I'm going for 10mm because its more common and there is no problem oversizing. All the radiators on the top row also only need 10 mm pipework. But it's the pipe that feeds them we need to concentrate on.

Below I have labelled how much heat goes down the main pipework, you just add up all the radiators downstream.15mm pipework would easily cope with this load.

When we are designing the system, this is the process we use. Its called indexing the pipework.

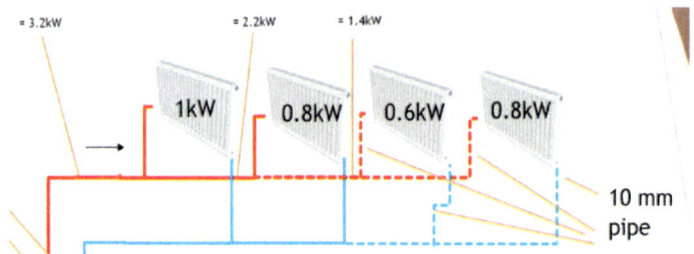

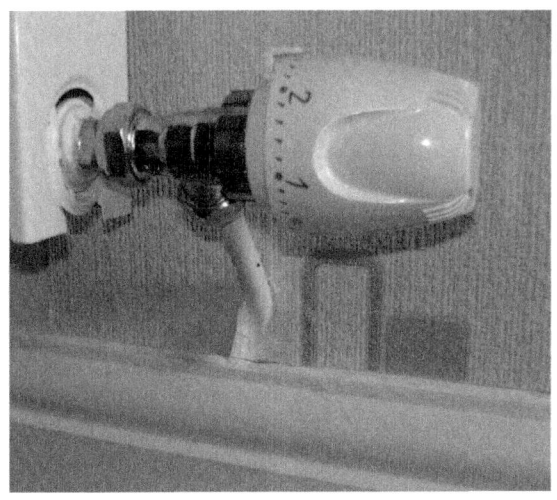

90 Does microbore work on heat pumps?

If you live in a house built in the 80s and 90s its highly likely your heating system has microbore pipework. You can easily tell if it's in your system, the pipe looks more like a cable, it's 10 or 12mm diameter and its often hidden in the walls almost as soon as it comes out the radiator. like the photo.

Ever week I hear someone say something as idiotic as microbore doesn't work on heat pumps. I have no idea who came up with this idea, but its rubbish. The pipe size is not a barrier to heat pump installation if you do a little bit of maths and design work.

In domestic installations no one sizes the pipework, we just use rules of thumb and pipe the house up as we like. If you think this is untrue think about this.......... In small rooms with small radiators, you need less water to heat the room so it should have small pipes. In big rooms with big radiators, you need more water, so the pipes should be bigger. Now check your house, I'm willing to bet that every radiator in the house has the same size pipework.

Modern Gas condensing boilers have very slow flow and very high temperatures. They deliver the water to the radiators at about 70 degrees C let it hang around in the radiators for quite a long time so it falls to 50 degrees C, before it returns to the boiler for re heating.

In Old boilers the flow rate was faster but still with very high temperatures. They delivered the water to the radiators at about 70 degrees C let it hang around for a short time, so it falls to 60 degrees C before it returns to the boiler for re heating.

And finally in heat pumps we have very fast flow rates but medium temperatures. They deliver the water to the radiators at about 52 degrees C, we let it hang around in the radiators for a few seconds, so it falls to 47 degrees C before it returns to the heat pump for re heating.

If you house was built in the 80s a new condensing boiler is easy to install, sling it in, the temperatures remain the same and the flow is slower, so the pipework is always going to be big enough. A heat pump might be harder though, if we replace an old or a new boiler the flow rate is going to go up, a lot. We might need bigger pumps or bigger pipes.

Bearing in mind that no one sized any pipe work in your house, It's possible that in some rooms the microbore you have installed is too big for the job and in others its sized about right. My job as a system designer is to see if I can use these pipes for heating using a heat pump. But its unlikely that you can buy an off the shelf beige box heat pump and simple replace your boiler with it using the same old radiators, pipework, and cylinder unless you are very lucky.

Now for the fun bit, working out heat capacity of pipework is dull. The formulas are easy, but we love to use ridiculous units to maximise the chance of getting errors. It should have been sorted out years ago but wasn't, so you have m^3 per hour, litres a minute, mm, metres etc to trip you up. So, I got bored, wrote a table in excel and produced a guide.

How big room will each pipe serve?								
year /pipe dia mm od	8 mm	10 mm	12 mm	15 mm	22 mm	28 mm	35 mm
pre 1918	9	16	24	38	117	141	218
1918-1970	11	19	29	46	141	169	262
1970-1990	12	20	31	49	151	182	281
1990-2000	14	23	34	54	167	201	311
2000-2010	19	32	48	76	234	282	436
2010-2016	25	41	62	99	306	367	569
2016-2020	32	53	80	126	391	469	727
2016-2020 with HRV	39	66	99	157	485	583	902

We could work out how much heat we can squeeze down the pipe work, and the maximum room size each pipe can serve.

You can see that that old microbore pipe of 10 mm outside diameter that you have in your 1980s house will serve a room of 20m^2 if you connect it to a heat pump. If you have a bigger room, you will need more than one radiator and more than one set of 10mm pipes. It's not very hard if it's broken down into a simple table.

91 What's DNO and have I got enough power in my house?

A DNO stands for **a distribution network operator**. They are companies that control all the towers, cables, and electricity distribution within their designated area. When you are looking to install a heat pump, you must complete a DNO application. Here:

https://www.energynetworks.org/operating-the-networks/connecting-to-the-networks

The cut out It's the big fuse if its old like this assume 60 Amps, If it's even older you have to assume 30 Amps

Modern cut outs have the size written on them.

There is more info here: https://www.energynetworks.org/assets/images/Resource%20library/LCT_Cut-Out%20Rating%20Guidance%20to%20EV-HP%20Installers%20v1.1.docx.pdf

You are supposed to calculate max demand. Most people add up the mcbs and divide by 3 so mine is 6 + 12 + 6 + 40 + 32 + 32 = 128

128/3 = 42.7A

Apply to connect or connect and notify

Each heat pump is either apply to connect (typically larger units over 10kW) in this case you have to complete the DNO before you connect up. This can lead to delays Or if its connect and notify you install first them fill in the DNO.

92 Who is my dno?

You can find out who your DNO is here https://www.energynetworks.org/operating-the-networks/whos-my-network-operator Enter your postcode

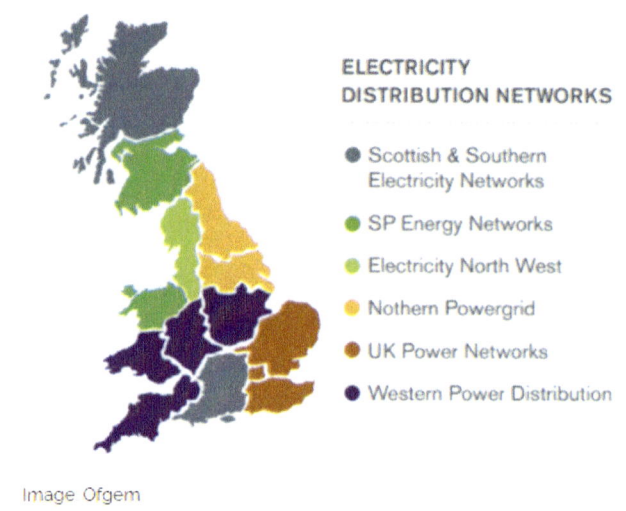

Image Ofgem

and it will tell you.

Or you can use the map here

Or Search "apply DNO" online:

My local DNO is SSE, here is a screen shot of the application form they like you to fill in.

Select the type of installation *

(•) Heat Pump ( ) EVCP

Premises Type *

(•) Residential House ( ) Residential Flat ( ) Commercial ( ) Public ( ) Other - pleas

Premises MPAN – this should be 13 digits beginning with 17 or 20. If you are unsure confirm here *

[13 digit MPAN or 11 digit MPRN]

Declared Voltage at Connection Point *

[Volts]

Number of Phases *

( ) Single Phase ( ) Split/two Phase ( ) Three Phase

Type of Metering at installation location *

( ) CT Metered ( ) Whole Current Metered

SSE has been contacted about the installation ? *

( ) Yes ( ) No

Import or load limiting device on premises *

( ) Yes ( ) No

Final or Proposed Earthing Arrangements *

( ) TN-C-S (PME) ( ) TN-S (SNE) ( ) TT (Direct) ( ) Customer Substation (HV CT met

Is the service looped? *

( ) Yes ( ) No ( ) Don't know

Have you identified any issues with adequacy of the existing supply equipment? *

( ) Yes ( ) No

Installation date

[📅]

93 Types of Supply

The DNO will ask what type of supply you have at home. You need to get a clear photo of the service fuse and the meter

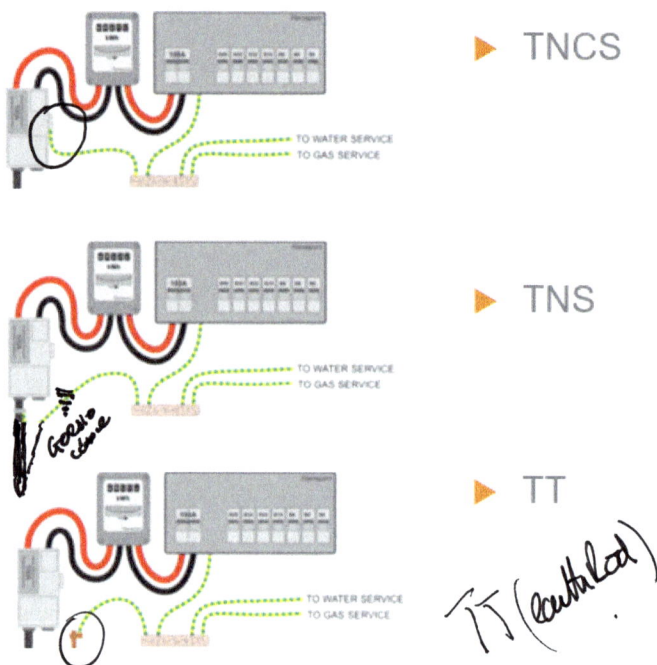

▶ TNCS

▶ TNS

▶ TT

and the cable coming out the ground.

The type of supply shows us where the green and yellow earth cable connects into the system see here.

TNCS stands for Earth (t for Earth or terra) Neutral, combined system.

Here the earth cable goes into the service fuse.

TNS stands for Earth Neutral sperate, the earth cable joins the main cable as it comes out the ground, it bypasses the service fuse.

TT is where the earth cable goes into a copper spike in the ground it goes nowhere near the mains cable coming out the ground

Looped supply

A looped supply is **when two properties share a single electricity service cable** coming out the ground they are most commonly found in terraced or semi-detached properties.

A looped supply is perfectly safe; however, it may need to be separated if one neighbour wants to install a heat pump

94 Load shedders and power limiters

An import or load limiting device is **a piece of hardware and/or software that limits the demand (i.e., the amount of current drawn) by a premises**. In the case of an EV charge point/Heat Pump, this can be thought of as an EV/HP curtailment scheme.

If you have a heat pump, an electric car charger and a cooker all running at the same time you can exceed the maximum power level for your house.

One solution is to put an intelligent switch on the power supply which limits the car charger or switches off the power to keep under the maximum current. This is load shedding.

We use load shedding devices to help us get through the DNO application and to protect the incoming mains cable.

95 Identifying my heating system.

Single Pipe:

Single pipe systems were popular in the 1950s and 196s they tubed it like this below. The radiators are connected to the same pipe in a loop round the house. The idea is that the hot water will rise into the radiators, cool and fall back into the pipe. The problem was the first radiator is very hot but as you go round the house the radiators get colder and colder. You often see lots of radiators in the rooms furthest from the boiler. They can be easy to spot, they didn't use TRVs on the

radiators with this system. If there are no trvs keep an eye out for single pipe.

You cannot use this system with a heat pump it doesn't work, we can't give you the temperature needed to make it work well.

The boiler will have 5 pipes connected, 2 for heating, 2 for the hot water cylinder and 1 for gas. There will not be any zone valves in the system.

To make matters worse the first rad was boiling hot, but by the end of the run the water had been thought a bunch of radiators so it was much colder. The last room on the loop tended to have lots of radiators, all of them were cold. No one does this anymore because it's awful.

I have tried a heat pump on my own single pipe system to see if it would work. It didn't. It was freezing, the rads didn't get warm but the primary loop of pipework was lovely and hot.

If you have a single pipe heating system in your house trust me, DONT BUY A HEATPUMP, or at least if you insist buy one have the house piped up properly.

A conventional Gas Combi boiler installation

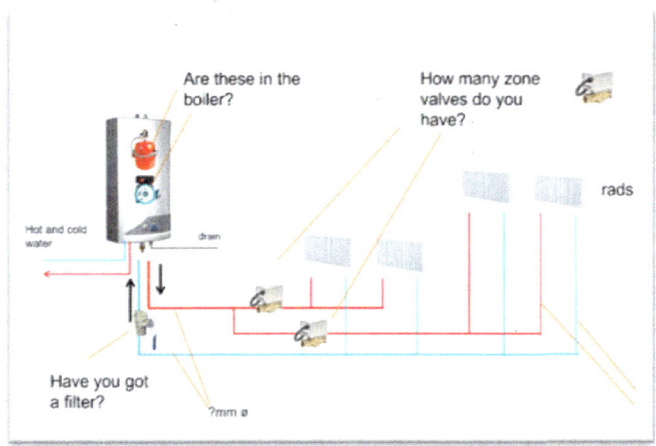

The most popular heating system in the UK is a combi system. Combi boilers make hot water instantly without a cylinder in the house. The boiler will have 6 or 7 pipes connected to it. 2 for hot water, 2 for heating, a safety drain, a plastic drain, and a gas pipe.

A conventional Gas system boiler installation with cylinder, S plan 2 x 2 port valves

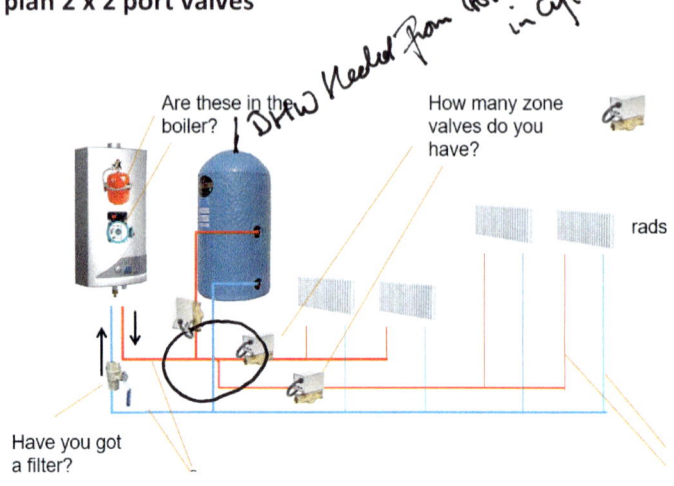

In the plumbing world we call this a system boiler installation, there is a hot water cylinder in the house. The boiler will have 3 or 4 pipes connected to it, a gas pipe, a drain and 2 heating pipes. The main heating and hot water pipes will have a 2-port valve to let the water up to the cylinder and another to let the hot water go out to the radiators and underfloor heating.

In big houses you can have more than 2 zone valves (2 ports) and thermostats, we need to know how many there are.

A conventional Gas system boiler installation Y plan - 3 port

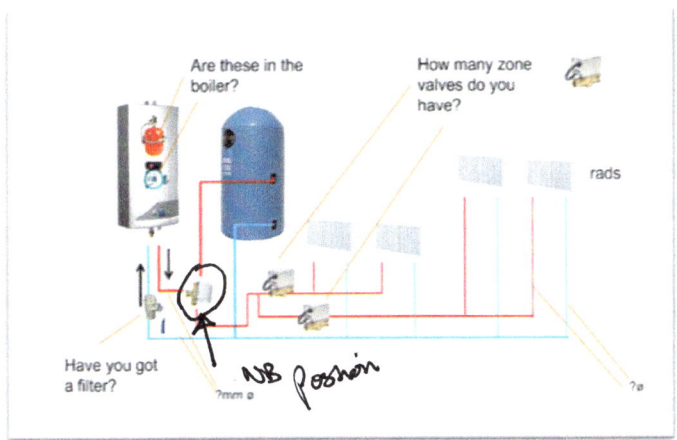

valve

In a system boiler installation, there is a hot water cylinder in the house. The boiler will have 3 or 4 pipes connected to it, a gas pipe, a drain and 2 heating pipes. The main heating and hot water pipes will have a 3-port valve to let the water up to the cylinder OR to the radiators and underfloor heating.

In big houses you can have more than 2 zone valves (2 ports) and thermostats, we need to know how many there are.

Information we require to identify your system:

When we are looking at your heating system, we like to get a photo of the old boiler and the connections too it.

We need a photo of the boiler data plate.

We need to know how many zone valves or thermostats you have in the house. We also need to find out where those 2 or 3 port zone valves are in the house, they may be hidden.

We need to know if you have a hot water cylinder, how big it is (data plate) and can you get to it?

But most importantly we need to know if you are currently warm and do you run out of hot water.

Installing a heat pump into a house with an already defective heating system is not a great plan.

96 What servicing will my heat pump need?

It's no longer mandatory under the boiler upgrade scheme to have a maintenance agreement but Heat pumps should normally be serviced once a year to maintain the warranty.

When taking up an annual service it should include:

Full clean of the ASHP unit, including removing any debris from the coil at the back.

Heating performance checks and removal of any trapped air

Checking that the system is adequately protected from frost (Glycol level)

Ensuring pressure & flow rates are correct

All system filters are clean

Checking all the controller settings and timers

Inspection of hot water and legionella protection settings and the G3 kit

97 What is going to go wrong with my heat pump and who can fix it?

Hopefully nothing will go wrong, remember your heat pump uses the same technology as your freezer.

When did your freezer last go wrong?

Like all mechanical devices if you leave it alone and don't tinker with it all the time it's likely to march on for years without failure.

It's a sealed system so most of the parts are maintenance free.

The most common issues are filters getting blocked because the water in the pipework is dirty.

Bad setup so the unit is not working to its best ability

The hot water tank sensor being pulled out of the cylinder

Water leaks in the system causing the pressure to drop

The Top 10 errors for heat pumps:

There are videos on YouTube telling you what these errors means and how to solve them.

- ▶ Flow rate low, dirty filters, air etc
- ▶ Power off to outdoor unit, dead controller
- ▶ Legionella failure
- ▶ Unit overheating
- ▶ Unit high pressure
- ▶ The Timers incorrectly set
- ▶ How to set the clock
- ▶ How to unlock the controller when its locked (padlock symbol)
- ▶ High run cost or high electric bills
- ▶ There is smoke coming out of my unit

98 My heat pump has frozen up, who defrosts it?

In cold, wet weather your heat pump will freeze. It's not uncommon for it too look like this after an hour of working hard.

It's completely normal. Remember it's just a freezer, so it needs regular defrosting.

Unlike your freezer you don't have to do this yourself, its automatic.

Once the unit detects that is frozen up it stops, reverses the heat pump cycle, and slightly warms the frozen coil. This happens a maximum once an hour and takes 6 minutes.

If your unit freezes badly like this one, where there is and the ice coming out past the casing something is very wrong with your unit, or your installation.

You need an engineer to come to site to test the system and see what's wrong. Something has gone wrong with the automatic defrosting.

The 3 main reasons for this to happen are:

The First reason is the unit is boxed in, so the air is going through the unit more than once, this is easy to measure, if its much colder at the back of the heat pump thank it is in the garden you have this issue.

The second reason is the unit is struggling to supply enough heat to your house, it could be undersized or underperforming.

In Winter your heat pump will freeze up, its normal.

When it defrosts the ice on the unit melts and drains out of the unit onto the floor.

The unit will produce 6 liters of water per hour.

This water is clean, it's not from the radiators its just the ice on the coil melting.

In these 3 photos taken 2 minutes apart you can see a unit going from frozen to clear.

At the end of the defrost cycle the coil will be slightly warm, when the fan starts up you often see a cloud of steam. Just like you can see your breath on cold days.

Its normal, don't worry, the unit is not on fire.

99 What refrigerant is in my heat pump are some better than others?

In 2015 our industry had a change of refrigerant, we lurched from R410A the refrigerant we had used very successfully for 15 years, to a new refrigerant R32. The reason it was done was R32 is a lot less damaging to the environment than the old gases. If your refrigerant were to leak into the air it has the same effect as discharging Co2 into the atmosphere, it causes global warming. So, we are keen to keep it inside the unit. The environmental lobby are also pushing us to use less damaging refrigerants so R32 was introduced to replace R410A.

R32 is a better refrigerant, it's better for the environment and it allows us to run heat pumps at higher temperatures but………. Its slightly flammable.

With R410A units the units started to run out of steam as the water temperature gets over 45C. In most R410A heat pumps we use an immersion heater to help get the last couple of degrees in the hot water tank, it's not ideal, but it works.

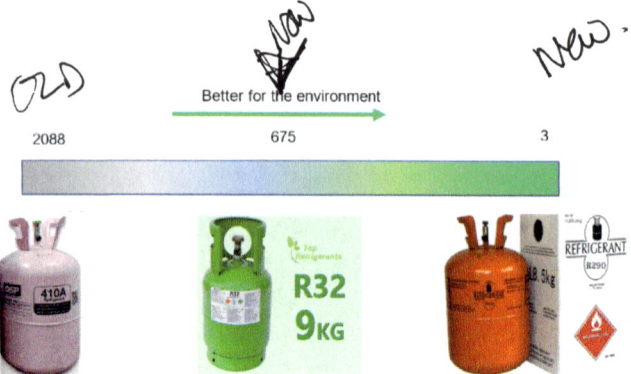

In 2022 most heat pumps use R32, but we are moving towards R290

With R32 its possible to push the unit to water temperatures of 60C so we can maintain a constant 10-degree temperature difference between the water in the tank and the water coming out the heat pump, the cylinder recovery never slows down. It means hotter water quicker. It's a lovely feature, it works well. In brief R32, it's like all the old gases but it's better for the environment and you can have a warmer shower quicker.

In 2022 we are due a new even greener refrigerant. The most popular new gas will be R290, its propane, the barbeque gas.

R290 is much less harmful to the environment if it leaks, but its very flammable. R290 also allows for even higher water temperatures. New units running at 75 degrees C and higher will be available with this new refrigerant

100 If the refrigerant is flammable, will it be dangerous?

See Q99

As the global warming potential of refrigerants fall and they become less damaging to the environment their flammability increases. This worries homeowners. You cannot have and do not want flammable gas in the house. No one stores their BBQ bottle in the house, but they are safe outside. It's the same for your heat pump.

The new refrigerant we are suing R290 is propane, it's the same as the gas in your BBQ gas bottle.

To protect you from fire there is a piece of legislation limiting the amount of flammable gas you can have running through the house, its called EN378 and it states a limit.

R-410A: 0.44 kg/m³,

R32 0.061kg/m³,

R290 0.008kg/m³

A 16kW heat pump contains 1.5kg of refrigerant

The smallest room it could go in is:

3.4 m³ for R410A

25 m³ for R32

187 m³ for R290

101 Why is my run cost higher in Winter than Summer?

Run cost estimation per month of heat pump		cost / month
Month	% energy used/ month	
January	19%	£ 235.06
February	17%	£ 210.31
March	12%	£ 148.46
April	7%	£ 86.60
May	4%	£ 49.49
June	2%	£ 24.74
July	1%	£ 12.37
August	1%	£ 12.37
September	4%	£ 49.49
October	6%	£ 74.23
November	12%	£ 148.46
December	15%	£ 185.57
total	100.00%	£ 1,237.14

12.37 kW*

All heating systems work harder in Winter than summer, that's obvious.

In this example you would pay a direct debit of £100 a month. In summer you are overpaying and winter you are underpaying. It averages out over the year.

If we plot the energy use per month on a graph you can see it's a sine wave.

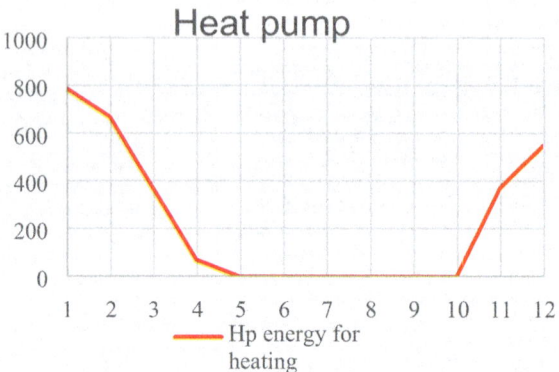

When it's cold, in January my heat pump runs continuously in Jan 22 it was running 71% of the time, that's because its set up properly. Heat pumps should be set to run all the time.

It's not uncommon for consumers to take their daily run figure in January and assume this will happen every day of the year. We get calls from people saying I'm using 55kWhrs of electricity a day at 30p a unit that's £16 a day if I multiply that by 365 days that's £6000 a year. My gas boiler was only £250 a month.

If you pay for your energy by direct debit, the suppliers average the usage over the year, so you pay a flat value, but you obviously use a lot more energy in Winter than Summer. The energy providers are making life easy for you. No one ever rings me in July to say, " I'm saving a fortune, the boiler used to cost £120 a month its now only using 3 units a day which is £1 a day, bargain".

But it gets more complicated than that, the graph above is an average over the month, it doesn't show you the peak value per day.

The average December temperature in Southampton is 6 degrees C. on this average day I will use 25 units a day, if its -1c I could easily use double that, if its 10C much less.

Don't panic if your run cost is high today, if its cold outside, keep an eye on it and take regular readings. Don't look at your direct debit, you need to look at actual use. If you bought your heat pump of someone reputable, they would have supplied it with dedicated meters that read just the heat pumps consumption. I'm not interested in your house consumption, what you do with your electricity at home is your business. In my house we use 6 kWhrs of electricity every day for lights, cooking internet etc. You could be using a lot more if you have security lights a tumble drier, kids etc.

18- m. view.

2.46.

About the Author:

Graham Hendra is a heat pump consultant working for ABC heat pumps limited.

He has been working in the renewable heat sector since 2008

He spends his time training, designing systems, writing manuals, and blogging about heat pumps on Linked In.

He feels the subject is not very complicated, it's just badly explained, he hopes this book helps.

Contact Graham on <u>Graham@abcHeatpumps.co.uk</u>

Printed in Great Britain
by Amazon